Yours till the end

bush
PUBLISHING
& associates

Foreword by
MAJOR GENERAL STEVEN N. WICKSTROM

A **WWII** *account of the*
42nd INFANTRY RAINBOW DIVISION
through the letters of Private Berlie Forehand

SHIRLEY FOREHAND KINSEY

Yours Till the End

A WWII Account of the 42nd INFANTRY RAINBOW DIVISION

Through the Letters of Private Berlie Forehand

Shirley Forehand Kinsey, Author

Tracie Maltezo, Cover and Layout Designer

The history recorded in this book was gathered from many sources by the author including: personal records, interviews, internet research, and *The 42nd Rainbow Infantry Division; A Combat History of World War II* By, Hugh C. Daly, Copyright 1946, Army and Navy Publishing Company, Baton Rouge, Louisiana.

Bush Publishing & Associates books may be ordered at www.bushpublishing.com or www.amazon.com. For further information, please contact:

Bush Publishing & Associates

www.bushpublishing.com

Library of Congress

ISBN 978-0-9824391-8-0

Printed in the United States of America

DEDICATION

This book is dedicated to my father, *Berlie Forehand*, who served his country in the United States Army during World War II. Every letter he wrote is the very foundation of this book.

And, in memory of my mother, *Hazel Fortner Forehand*, the recipient of the letters, without her careful preservation of each one, this book might not have been possible.

At last, to the *42nd Rainbow Infantry Division* that my father was so proud to have been a part of. Even 60 years later, he remembered events with such detail, shedding light on what it was like to be an infantryman, a doughboy, a foot soldier in World War II.

A portion of the proceeds from the sale of this book are being donated to the Rainbow Division Veterans Memorial Foundation.

ACKNOWLEDGMENTS

Special Thanks

The author, Shirley Forehand Kinsey, would like to thank retired U.S. Army Major General Joseph J. Taluto for his invaluable input on the assignments and accomplishments of the 42nd Infantry Rainbow Division during the years since World War II. Major General Taluto retired in February 2010 from a 44 year military career. He served as Joint Task Force Commander during the 42nd Infantry Division's initial emergency response to assist New York City in its security and recovery operations following the terrorist attacks on the World Trade Center. He commanded the 42nd Infantry Division from 2004-2006, as well as Task Force Liberty, during its deployment to Iraq in support of Operation Iraqi Freedom. My sincere thanks to you, General Taluto, for your many years of leadership in service to our great nation.

FOREWORD

As you walk into the 42nd Division Headquarters in Troy, New York, you will see the photographs, paintings and other images of the heroics of "Rainbow" soldiers throughout the years. These include a photo of Thomas Neibaur receiving the Medal of Honor in February 1919 in Chaumont, France from General John J. "Blackjack" Pershing. There is also a mural commemorating the 42nd's liberation of the Dachau concentration camp during World War II, as well as a large photograph of Lieutenant General Mark Clark inspecting the division soldiers during the occupation of Austria. Further down the hallway toward the commanding general's office, you will find a painting depicting the 1st Battalion 69th Infantry's taming of Route Irish, the main supply route into Baghdad. Nearby this painting, is a photo of Major Terry Meltz providing medical care to a group of Iraqi children. Then, at the end of the hallway, directly outside the division commander's office, are portraits of each of the twenty-three preceding division commanders. The 42nd Division has always had great leaders including, Charles T. Menoher from the First World War, Harry J. Collins of the Second World War, and Joseph J. Taluto of the Operation Iraqi Freedom. I am sure that each of them, even the most famous among them, Douglas MacArthur, would say that all glory belongs to the soldiers of the division.

This book, this compilation of letters dutifully written by mortarman, Berlie Forehand, were carefully and lovingly assembled by his daughter, Shirley, demonstrates all that has been great about "Rainbow" soldiers for the past ninety-five years. These soldiers had a willingness to travel far from home, endure hardship and risk great danger—all in an effort to protect those they loved at home and for a Nation based on the best ideals. Quite often, Army Chief of Staff, General Raymond T. Odierno has said, *"The strength of the Nation is our Army. The strength of our Army is our soldiers. The strength of our soldiers are our families.*" I strongly believe this is true. Berlie Forehand's letters are a testament that it has always been true.

Members of the division wear a rainbow patch as our unit designation. The patch is a tribute to our legacy and composition as an organization made from units in many States. After World War I, 42nd Division soldiers cut the patch in half to honor the one-half of their number that never made it home. After the Second World War, rainbowers like Burly Forehand did all they could to ensure the exploits of the 42nd Division soldiers would be forever remembered. In the 42nd Division, we greet each other by saying, *"Rainbow."* After the attacks on 11 September 2001, we adopted a new response to this greeting. We say, *"Never Forget."* This collection of letters written by Burly Forehand, and the efforts of his daughter, Shirley Forehand Kinsey, to publish them, is one of the reasons we will "never forget".

MG Steven N. Wickstrom
CG, 42nd Infantry Division
8 July 2012

TABLE OF CONTENTS

A Letter from the Author

Berlie Forehand and Hazel together the day after Berlie returned home December 1945.

It would be safe to say that millions of letters have been mailed to and from members of the United States Armed Forces during the last century. For the cause of freedom, both our own and that of other nations as well, we have been involved in several wars: World War I, World War II, the Korean War, the Vietnam War, the Gulf War, the War in Iraq and Afghanistan, besides other conflicts to which our troops have been sent. For most of the century, correspondence was by mail, and great care was taken to assure that letters made it to their destinations. There is no way to know how many of those letters were kept and how many were not, or perhaps were lost in moves, disposing of estates, or still lie undiscovered in attics and closets. So when a stack of letters written over a half-century ago is found, carefully preserved and in the same condition in which they were received, it is like unveiling a piece of history, a personal connection of personalities with important world events.

The letters upon which this book is based lay hidden away, basically untouched, for several decades, and were only discovered after the death and burial of the lady who had safeguarded them so well. The lady was my mother, and the letters were written to her by my father while he was serving in the United States Army's 42nd Infantry Rainbow Division in 1944-45 in Europe. After I read those letters, I somehow knew that this was a story that needed to be told.

And as I wrote, I found that it was not only what was in the lines, but what, and who, was "behind the lines" that captured my interest and propelled me forward with this book. Any writer will tell you that the story almost writes itself as you become absorbed in the telling of it. You feel the cold, you hear the shells flying through the air, you see the destruction taking place before your very eyes, you smell the fire and smoke, and you sense the relief of finally getting a hot shower and fresh food after days of dirt and sweat and k-rations.

It is my hope that you also find yourself absorbed in the history and personal reflections of this true depiction of an infantryman's perspective of his involvement in World War II.

Shirley Forehand Kinsey

Berlie Forehand and Shirley Forehand Kinsey make the news after Shirley published the letters written by her dad during WWII. Right, The silk french pouch the letters Berlie's wife, Hazel, stored in for more than 50 years.

Forehand family reunion before Berlie left for Europe.

Forehand, above, before going to basic training and with his young family and wife, Hazel, and daughters, Janice and Peggy.

Left, *General Douglas MacArthur (26 January 1880–5 April 1964).* Center, *General Douglas MacArthur, photo inscribed to Admiral Nimitz.* Right, *Major General Joseph J. Taluto, retired.*

Left, *Commanding General Major General Steven N. Wickstrom.* Center, *Sergeant Arnold Owen.* Right, *Forehand in Paris–1945.*

15

Left, Center, *Forehand, company barber, Germany.* Right, *Forehand playing the guitar in Austria.*

Top left, *Sgt. (Sarge) Owen.* Top right, *Chiem Sea, Germany from left to right: Forehand, Troger, Eaton, and Popio.* Right, Forehand visiting the Eiffel Tower and the Rainbow Handbook.

Top left: *April 1945 Capture of the Nazi flag in Rain, Germany.* Left to Right: *Eaton (Massachusetts), Forehand (Florida), Popio (Jeep driver from Ohio), Fine (Tennessee). Top right, Sarge and Forehand, retirement years.*

Above, Forehand on the way to Munich via Dachau. Right, Forehand enjoying his chow. Below, 1945 Paris sightseeing tour.

Forehand, after the war with his family and wife, Hazel. Left to Right: *Jerry, Shirley, Janice, Peggy, Frances. c. 1952*

Forehand Hazel in later years.

CHAPTER ONE

The Letters

Found under some gloves and scarves in the bottom drawer of the dresser of our mother's bedroom, was a yellow silk pouch. One side was imprinted with an American flag and only 48 stars. On the other side, a large red rose and the word "Wife". In the upper left hand corner, an eagle held in his talons, a shield of stripes and 13.

It was only the Sunday before that we had laid our beloved mother to rest in the cemetery just down the road. And now, since some of the children . . . five daughters and their families . . . had long drives ahead of them, we began the sad but necessary task of removing Mother's clothing and personal possessions from the house . . . knowing it would be hard for our dad to deal with such painful details alone.

We took out suits and dresses, shoes and purses—all those things women accumulate over so many years. Mama would have celebrated her seventy-fifth birthday in this house—the home our parents built and lived in together for more than twenty years.

Some things, like framed artwork, whatnots, vases, etc., were labeled on the back or bottom of the piece with our names in Mama's familiar handwriting. Those things were easy to separate into piles. Others were not so easy so we drew numbers in order to be fair to one another. The special "Sunday" china—gilt-edged and pink flowers was divided into place settings and each of us placed pieces into our growing pile of memorable treasures. We did the same with the special silverware, antique bowls and dishes, and the large collection of dainty porcelain and glass shoes that Mama had lovingly collected for years.

Dad had suggested that all four of his daughters and his only daughter-in-law divide Mom's special possessions. He told us, "I won't be needing all of these things, so you girls can take them and use them . . . that's what your Mama would have wanted". So, we began removing items from the cabinets and shelves. Daddy mostly stayed away from the house checking on his business or working in the garage. We knew how difficult this was for him. After all, they had been married for fifty-six years.

When sifting through the possessions left behind by someone you loved, everything that belonged to them, everything they touched, suddenly seems more precious. A lacy handkerchief, a book, a beloved pocket watch or piece of jewelry, or a faded photograph—each, no matter how small, takes on new significance and value, and seems in some way to be a small part of the person left to remind us that they were here. Later, even years later, seeing those same things brings back memories of that person.

And now, from out of the past, and from the bottom of a lingerie drawer, we discovered a part of Mama she had kept hidden away for more than fifty years.

As the silk pouch was held up for all to see, there were exclamations: "Look!" "What is that?" "I've never seen that before!" "Are those Daddy's war letters?" We all sat down on the carpet beside the dresser and, almost reverently, opened the soft silk pouch. Realizing that we had discovered a very personal possession that had for so many years been safely hidden, we could hardly contain our excitement and tears. On the inside of the pouch, in beautiful calligraphy and surrounded by a frame of red roses, we read a poem of eight lines:

TO MY WIFE

Wife of my heart, it is you
You make my life so complete
You make all my dreams come true
So loving so loyal so sweet
Sharing each laugh and each tear
Faithful and true to the end
To me you will always be dear
My sweetheart, my partner, my friend.

We pulled out the letters—there were sixty-nine of them. The first letter, "At Sea" was dated November 30, 1944. Although the pouch was not large, maybe only six by nine inches, it was large enough to hold all the letters since most of them were V-Mail; reduced to a

size much smaller than the originals. Since the platoon officers were responsible for reading over the letters, they were stamped and signed by the officer that had censored them. In a few instances, a couple of words were blacked out, but the letters were all in perfect condition … every letter was carefully folded in the original creases.

Each of us took a letter and began reading. It was as if we were opening pages of our past that we had been slightly aware of. We had seen the small black and white photos that Dad had sent Mama during the war, or had brought back with him, but this was more. Reading these letters was like feeling the same emotions Dad felt when leaving behind his young wife who was six months pregnant and two young daughters. It was like experiencing for ourselves the seasickness, the homesickness, and the fatigue of a soldier, husband, and father at war, but at the same time, the courage of a young soldier and the desire to ease Mama's worries about him. The letters contained continual expressions of the hope of returning home to his family . . . even a sketch of the house he planned to build for them upon his return home. Many of the letters were numbered while others were not. But, by the dates written at the top of each one, it seemed that a few letters were missing. Perhaps they never had arrived.

While we sat on the carpet pouring over the letters, Dad quietly walked into the bedroom. Excitedly, we held up the letters for him to see saying, "Daddy, look what we found! Your war letters to Mama!"

As he stood there looking at the silk pouch and the letters in our hands, tears filled his blue eyes and rolled down his cheeks, "I didn't know she had kept those", he said. His voice choking on the words, "Where did you find them?" We pointed Mama's bottom dresser drawer. "Under the scarves and things," we told him. He lovingly picked up the silk pouch and a handful of letters off the bed and spoke his thoughts aloud, "Why didn't she tell me she had kept them? Why didn't she ever take them out? I wish I had known they were here. I sent her the silk pouch from Paris . . . haven't seen it all these years".

But behind his words of wonder, we sensed a deep satisfaction—a knowing that the letters had meant so much to Mama that she had tenderly tucked them away, never telling anyone about them. Seeing the letter he had written seemed to settle a long forgotten question in his mind, even in his heart.

Fifty-one years had passed since Daddy had written the last of the letters . . . the last one being dated November 10, 1945.

V-mail from Forehand to his wife and family.

CHAPTER TWO

Childhood, Romance, Marriage

Berlie and Hazel began their married life when both were only 18 years old, two young people who grew up in the country in the Florida Panhandle during the years of the Great Depression. Hazel's father, Mitchell Fortner, died when she was only nine years old, leaving her mother, Belle, to raise their six daughters and four sons. The last son, Joe Richard, weighed only two pounds at birth, according to Hazel, and could fit into a coffee can. With no real medical attention at all, he survived and grew into a strong healthy man. After Grandpa Mitch died at age 55, Granny Belle never remarried. It took all of her time and energy just to clothe and feed her brood of ten.

The older boys took jobs cutting timber, farming, and working turpentine to help provide for the younger ones. The family planted a vegetable garden, and Granny Belle and the girls preserved the harvest in canning jars. The chickens they raised provided them with fresh eggs and meat, and the smokehouse that stood in the side yard was used to preserve pork from the hogs they butchered every fall when the weather turned cold.

The children walked to the nearest school house, carrying their lunches in syrup tins filled with biscuits left from breakfast and a slice of meat left from supper the night before. Life was not easy, but life went on, and they each helped make the best of it; quilting and sewing, planting and harvesting, canning and preserving, studying and working, washing and hanging, and ironing the clothes. In such a large family, there were not many quiet moments. On Sundays, Granny Belle took the children to services at the Cypress Creek Missionary Baptist Church.

Berlie, born in 1921, was number six out of nine children born to Grandpa Ruel Elijah Forehand and Grandma Dollie. They moved from place to place in the Florida Panhandle, wherever Grandpa could get work, mostly cutting timber, farming, or working in the turpentine business. Each time they moved, the first thing Grandma Dollie did was scrub the walls and floors of the house with lye soap and hot water till she felt the house was clean enough to unpack their belongings and set up housekeeping.

These were the days of the Depression, and money was hard to come by, so many young boys began working at an early age to add to the family income. Berlie left school at the age of twelve to work, going along with his father and older brothers to whatever job they were working at. At age 16, he earned 35 cents an hour on a construction job building the Blountstown-Bristol Bridge which replaced the ferry that had long been in use. Although Dad often told us how he wished he could have finished school, we always admired how he carried on with his own education, always reading and learning new things, having a thirst for knowledge and highly motivated to be successful.

In 1939 Dad traveled to California and worked for several months with the federal government's RDA program. He was back home in Florida cutting cypress and pine posts for tobacco farmers to use when he met Hazel. Berlie's family was living in the same area of the country as Hazel's family when someone introduced them. They were both 18 years old; Hazel was a senior at Kinard High School and played on the girls basketball team. On their first date, they went to see the movie "For Me and My Gal" at the Eagle theater in Blountstown, twenty miles away.

When Hazel graduated and they decided to marry, a friend of Dad's carried him and Hazel in a logging truck to the county courthouse in Blountstown. There they made their wedding vows before the judge, signed their wedding license, and climbed back into the logging truck for the ride home, thus beginning fifty-six years of life together.

It was the year 1940, and the Second World War was already in progress across the Atlantic Ocean. Paris had fallen to the Germans on June 14, and German soldiers had planted giant swastika flags at the Arc d' Triomphe and on top of the Eiffel Tower. But it would be almost another year and a half before the United States would be drawn into the war, with the Dec. 7, 1941 Japanese attack on Pearl Harbor, Hawaii, followed by President Franklin D. Roosevelt's urging the United States Congress to declare a state of war between the United States and the Empire of Japan. And only four days later, on Dec. 11, Germany's Adolf Hitler declared war on the United States. Though all too real

when the news was announced on radio broadcasts and newspaper headlines, it still seemed a world away.

CHAPTER THREE

World War II—How It All Began

It was 1940, and across the Atlantic Ocean, Germany's Adolf Hitler and Italy's Mussolini were waging war in Europe in a determination to expand their rule by conquering and taking over surrounding countries. Hitler had spent the last several years rapidly building up the German army and navy. He violated the Treaty of Versailles by moving German troops into the Rhineland, a German area on the border with France. In 1938 he had seized Austria, and in 1939 he had seized all of Czechoslovakia. Hitler knew he would have to deal with England and

France and referred to them as "two hateful enemies" in one of his fiery speeches, knowing that, to them, a strong Germany in the center of Europe would not be tolerated. He said: "There must be a final settlement with France in a last desperate struggle. Germany must regard the destruction of France as a means which will give our German people the chance to expand elsewhere".

Then in September of 1939 Hitler sent German war planes and tanks to invade Poland, in what was known as the blitzkrieg or "lightning war". This was only a week after Germany had signed a nonaggression treaty with the Soviet Union; a couple of weeks later, the Russians also invaded Poland. Hitler had earlier made the statement, in reference to Germany's need for raw materials: "If I had the Ural Mountains, with their great stores of treasure in raw materials, and if I had Siberia, with its vast forests; and the Ukraine, with its tremendous wheat fields; then Germany under my leadership would swim in plenty". It was obvious that regardless of any treaty he might sign, Hitler's greed for power and territory would not stop until he had even the Soviet Union under his control. He also said: "Our people will never be able to obtain the land we need for our existence as a favor from other countries. We will have to win these things by the power of a victorious sword".

During 1940, the Germans invaded Denmark and Norway, Belgium, Netherlands and Luxembourg; on June 10, Italy declared war on Britain and France. On June 3 and 4, waves of German bombers had flown over Paris and dropped an estimated 1000 bombs. The Parisians could not believe it was happening; they loaded up a few possessions in anything they could travel in and began leaving the city, going south on the few roads that were still open. So many fled that the city was almost empty when the Germans arrived on June 14 and German soldiers planted huge swastika flags at the Arc d'Triomphe and on top of the Eiffel Tower. On July 10 Germany attacked Britain, beginning the Battle of Britain, and began bombing London on September 7. On December 15, the British forces drove the Italian army out of Egypt.

The year 1941 saw a further escalation of aggression on the part of the Axis Powers, as Germany, Italy and Japan were called. At the end of March, Hitler's Afrika Korps launched a counteroffensive in North Africa, and in April, Nazi forces invaded Greece and Yugoslavia. In May the Germans invaded the British-held island of Crete in the eastern Mediterranean. On June 22 Germany declared war on the Soviet Union and launched an invasion on a 1000 mile front, from the Baltic to the Black Sea. On September 8, the Germans completed the land encirclement of Leningrad, starting a 900-day siege of the city, and a week or so later they also occupied Kiev, the capital city of Soviet Ukraine.

Across the Pacific Ocean, while Hitler and Mussolini were invading their neighbors in Europe, Japan was also preparing for conquests in Asia. Deciding that the road to political power and material prosperity lay in expanding onto the mainland of Asia, Japan began to pursue this path of aggression in 1931 by seizing Manchuria, a part of northeastern China. A state of war with China followed, which virtually gave the Japanese military control of the Japanese government. They savagely drove out Chinese military forces from Shanghai, and when a report condemning the Japanese action in Manchuria was presented by the appointed Lytton Commission, Japan withdrew from the League of Nations.

For the next several years the Japanese military continued to control Japan's government. Government officials who did not go along with the military were targeted for assassination. When Japan further invaded China, and a conference was held in Brussels in 1937 with nineteen nations participating, Japan refused to send delegates to discuss ending the war. From 1937 to 1941, Japan only became more aggressive. Even plainly marked American schools, hospitals, and churches were bombed in China, and the American gunship USS Panay was sunk and her survivors were deliberately shot down.

Finally in July of 1939, when the Japanese bombed an American church near the US Embassy in Chungking, and close to another American gunboat, President Roosevelt imposed trade sanctions on Japan. Diplomatic negotiations were tried, but it became clearer all the time that the Japanese militarists would not be stopped in their quest for expansion. On July 26, 1941, The United States ordered the freezing of all Japanese assets in the United States and imposed limitations on trade with Japan, forbidding the shipment of any U.S. oil to Japan. Japanese militarists, led by General Hideki Tojo, angrily called for greater war preparations. The premier of Japan tried to reach an agreement with the United States, but finally resigned in October of 1941, and General Tojo became premier. With his propaganda, the anti-American campaign was intensified; there were even warnings of a possible Japanese attack on the United States. Japan sent representatives to Washington for "peace" talks, but demanding that the United States remove the trade limitations, stop giving aid to China, and recognize Japan's political dominance in Asia. The United States demanded that Japan withdraw from China, recognize China's independence, sign a pact of nonaggression with all the powers in the Pacific area, and withdraw from its alliance with Hitler and Mussolini; Japan had signed a friendship treaty with Germany and Italy a year earlier. Hitler's Nazism and Japan militarists' policy had a lot in common, both eager to expand their empires at any cost.

Japanese forces poured into Southeast Asia on December 6, and on the next day, Sunday, December 7, with the Japanese envoy still in Washington preparing more peace talks, the Japanese made a surprise attack on the United States Pacific fleet at Pearl Harbor, Hawaii. Ships were sunk, a tremendous amount of military equipment was lost, and the loss of human lives was staggering; the numbers climbed higher and higher in the aftermath, with 2,343 dead, more than 1,200 wounded, and nearly 1,000 missing. President Roosevelt was immediately notified, and his response was quick; on Monday the 8th he urged Congress to declare a state of war between the United States and the Empire of Japan. The President read the statement of declaration of war in a radio message to the nation:

"Yesterday, December 7, 1941—a date which will live in infamy— the United States of America was suddenly and deliberately attacked by naval and air forces of the empire of Japan." He went on to say that even while Japanese government representatives had been delivering a formal reply to the Secretary of State concerning a recent American message, Japanese bombers had already begun the attack on Oahu. It was obvious the attack had been planned for some time before and the Japanese were only deceiving the Americans with hopes of a peaceful solution. Besides the attack on Pearl Harbor, the Japanese had already begun attacks on Malaya, Hongkong, Guam, Philippine Islands, Wake Island, and Midway Island, and had torpedoed American ships between San Francisco and Hawaii. The President concluded his radio speech with the words, "We will gain the inevitable triumph—so help us God". Shortly after his radio message, the Congress adopted a resolution declaring war on Japan, and three hours later Roosevelt signed the declaration of war.

Front-page headlines declared our nation at war with Japan: "U.S. DECLARES WAR; PACIFIC BATTLE WIDENS; MANILA AREA BOMBED"; and the next day: "ROOSEVELT PREDICTS A LONG WORLD-WIDE WAR".

On December 11, only four days after the attack on Pearl Harbor, Germany's Adolf Hitler declared war on the United States, and in turn Roosevelt asked for and received from Congress a declaration of war against Germany and Italy.

So now, a decade after Japan's invasion of Manchuria and twenty-seven months after Hitler's invasion of Poland, the United States was going to war, the bloodiest war ever fought. This war would cover more land and sea, and end with a greater total loss of lives, than any other war.

Of 90 million people who would be involved in this great war, nearly a fifth of them, or 17 million, would die, besides the cost in civilian lives. A staggering number, because this war would not be confined to one small country; the fighting would be spread over many countries in Europe and Asia and Africa, and would leave in its wake incredible destruction and loss of life.

And now , with the entrance of the United States into the war, would begin four years of hard work and sacrifice on the part of millions of Americans, all doing their part, large or small, to defeat the enemy, liberate conquered peoples and nations, and raise the banner of freedom on the other side of the world.

Most of the ships of the U.S. Pacific Fleet had been destroyed at Pearl Harbor; now U.S. Shipyards would work around the clock producing more carriers, battleships, cruisers, destroyers, submarines, and other combat vessels, besides thousands of other ships.

And while the men of the armed forces were shipping out for the war, Americans on the home front went to work producing war materials, and sacrificing many of their pleasures and even necessities in order that the men on the battlefields would have whatever they needed to come home victorious from this war. War bonds were sold to help finance the war, and Americans bought billions of dollars worth of the war bonds in support of their country. They waited in lines with ration cards to purchase their allowed quantities of foods, clothing, and gasoline. Nylon was needed for parachutes, so women used leg makeup instead, even using eye pencils to draw a fake seam up the back of each leg. Air raid practices were held in public schools, and street lights in Pacific coast cities were painted brown on the ocean side, so as not to be seen by Japanese submarines. Automobile tires were even rationed, and production of automobiles gave preference to production of aircraft and ships. Family by family, they participated in a nationwide effort to help their husbands, fathers, brothers, sons, uncles and nephews win this great war. Women joined the work force in record numbers in factories that produced the nuts and bolts, weapons and uniforms, vehicles, planes, and foods needed on the battlefield.

Families worked, saved, and sacrificed together, for their men, for their nation, and for freedom.

CHAPTER FOUR

From Home Building to Ship Building

For Berlie and Hazel, setting up a household as newlyweds in 1940 didn't take a lot of time. Their possessions were few and simple; a small poplar wood table and four chairs, a four-burner wood stove and a metal spring and bedstead with a roll-up mattress. They made a visit to Hill's General Store in Kinard and announced they had just married and were there to make a few purchases. Having only a few dollars to spend, they bought a big bag of   flour, some salt, and other staple goods. Hazel had been helping cook since she was nine years old, so she knew what she needed to have on hand to put a meal together. Mrs. Hill went through the store gathering up things, and presented the newlyweds with a flat iron skillet, a flour sifter, and a set of colored crockery bowls to help them set up housekeeping. With only a few other items given by family and friends, they were off to a good start. They first moved into an empty house owned by a turpentine company, and soon afterwards into a house not far from Granny Belle's, where they paid 50 cents a week for rent.

When Berlie's work took him farther away, he and Hazel moved into a little house "built over the water" on the Gulf of Mexico in Port St.. Joe, sharing the house with one of Berlie's brothers and his wife. That arrangement, however, didn't work out as well as they had hoped; and so they decided to move back to the area where they had started out.   There they tore down and then rebuilt a small wooden frame house, which Berlie affectionately dubbed the "shack". It was a three-room "shotgun house" of six-inch lap siding, with a hand pump for water on the back porch and a two-seat toilet out back in an outhouse. The "shack" was their home for the next five years.

During their first three years of marriage, Hazel gave birth to two daughters, first Peggy and then Janice. Berlie worked for a while at Eglin Air Force base a couple of hours' drive away, where he rented a room and shared a bath with another family. He missed being home with his family, so he found a job nearer home, earning 105 dollars a month driving a truck hauling soldiers in training at Tyndall Field, where one of seven gunnery schools in the country trained thousands of students in aerial gunnery. He hitchhiked a ride to and from home daily, and on several occasions when he was unable to catch a ride, he bedded down for the night in an empty building, rising early the next morning to get back to work, hoping to be able to make it home that evening. In October of '42 a job opened for him at the shipyard in Panama City, cutting huge sheets of thick metal with a blowtorch for the construction of Liberty Ships being used in the war. To make the daily drive back and forth from the little house in Kinard, he bought a 1937 Chevrolet for two hundred and twenty-five dollars cash and hauled five passengers who each paid him one dollar a day. The five dollars covered the cost of gas for the car and even left him a little for other expenses—no more hitchhiking for him, and he could count on sleeping in his own bed every night.

They were still living in the little rebuilt house and Berlie was still working at the shipyard when, in May of 1944, he received his draft notice from Uncle Sam which instructed him to report to Camp Blanding, near Jacksonville, Florida. He rode the bus with other young inductees to Camp Blanding where they all enlisted in the United States Army and were given two week's notice to report to Fort McPherson in Atlanta. On the day he enlisted, he bought his first uniform. Berlie knew he would be sent away to the war that raged on the other side of the world; he didn't know yet whether he would cross the Atlantic Ocean or the Pacific, but he knew he was willing to serve his country wherever his country needed him. Having been involved in the war effort on his last three jobs, he would now be going from his homeland to become involved in the war itself; he, along with millions of other young men, from a number of nations.

When the two weeks had passed and he had taken care of as many details as he could around home, Berlie rode from Blountstown with a bus load of other enlistees to Fort McPherson, Georgia, on May 19.

When his dog tags were cut and he noticed that his name was misspelled, with a "u" rather than an "e" in Berlie, and he brought their attention to it, he was told "Well, that's how it's spelled from now on." He nodded "Yes, sir", and from that time began spelling his name Uncle Sam's way. From Fort McPherson he was sent for Basic

Training to Camp Croft, in Spartanburg, South Carolina for sixteen weeks. As the train approached Camp Croft, Berlie watching from the window could see soldiers climbing the hills and thought "That's what I'll be doing". The new enlistees unloaded in the Camp, were assigned quarters and began the weeks of training. He was assigned to the 129th Infantry Training Battalion, and Berlie soon learned the rules, rigors and regulations of becoming a foot soldier; as they marched, ran, climbed, crawled, in the rain, in the mud, over and under obstacles. He was glad he was accustomed to strenuous work; training was tough but it had to be; they had to be strong physically and mentally for the rigors of war. They came from the north, the south, the east and the west; country boys and city boys alike, southern drawls and Yankee accents thrown together, but all training together for one purpose, to help win this war.

Not knowing how long he would be away from his family once he was sent away to war, and wanting to have as much time with them as possible, Berlie rented a furnished house for twenty dollars a month, and asked his brother Doris to drive Hazel and their two little girls to Spartanburg to spend his remaining months with him. Doris drove them up in the '37 Chevy, then Berlie bought a bus ticket to send his brother back to Florida. Berlie invited other young soldiers to their home for meals and invited two other couples to accompany his family on a Sunday afternoon drive to see Chimney Rock. The weeks of basic passed too quickly by, and when his time of training was over, Berlie drove Hazel and the girls back to their little house in Florida and helped settle them back in, then spent a couple of weeks getting things in order and saying his good-byes to their families.

Around the first of November, he hugged and kissed Hazel who was now over 7 months pregnant, and their two little girls Peggy and Janice, promised them he would return, then boarded the bus which took him to Marianna. There he, along with other young soldiers off to war, lifted his bag and climbed on board the train. After all the tension of trying to leave things in order at home and saying goodbye to his family, he could at least settle back and try to relax on the long train ride to Camp Gruber, Oklahoma. Looking out the coach window, he thought about the train ride he had made to California with the CCC in '39, and how different that ride had been from this trip. This trip was more than a job, more than an adventure; this trip was his patriotic duty. As the train cars clicked over the rails heading west, the young soldier began to feel the distance separating him from home and family. He wouldn't hear anyone calling him "Daddy", "Dada", as baby Jan called him, or even "Berlie" for a long time; he would now answer to Private Berlie Forehand. Tucked away in his bag was an 8x10 photo he and Hazel and the two girls had made in a studio on the day he bought his first uniform; he planned to keep the photo near, no matter where this war took him, it would make him feel closer to them and remind him of all the reasons he had to make it back home after this war was over. He knew that many soldiers had already died and many others were wounded or missing in the war he was headed for; he would proudly serve his country along with millions of other soldiers, and hopefully he would be one of the lucky ones to make it back home some day.

A number of other soldiers were on the train with Forehand, and they were friendly with one another, going to meals in the dining car together, talking about their homes and families. The train rolled on as darkness fell, and Forehand settled down as comfortably as he could, then fell asleep to the steady clatter of the train wheels on the steel tracks.

The early morning sun shining in the window woke him up. He was hungry, and after a trip to the toilet where he splashed cold water on his face and combed his hair, he went to the dining car and found a seat at a table with several other soldiers. After a hot breakfast and coffee, they returned to their coach seats and talked quietly to each other or sat gazing out the window lost in their own thoughts.

The day wore on, and as the train took him farther and farther away from home and family, Forehand knew he would face some lonesome days ahead. He was a soldier; he felt the pride and responsibility a soldier feels; but he had a lot of questions in his mind; where would he

end up going, what was it like to be up front in a battle. His thoughts were interrupted as the train slowly ground to a stop. They had finally arrived at Camp Gruber; Forehand hoisted his bag and followed the other young soldiers down the aisle and out onto the platform where they were met and escorted to their barracks.

In Camp Gruber, Oklahoma, Private Burlie Forehand joined the 42nd Rainbow Infantry Division.

CHAPTER FIVE

Off to War Again

The 42nd Rainbow Division was formed when America entered into World War I and the government decided to create a division composed of hand-picked national guard units from 26 states and the District of Columbia. The division was organized in September, 1917 at Camp Mills on Long Island, New York. When Col. Douglas McArthur, who helped form the division, said "The 42nd Division stretches like a rainbow from one end of America to the other", the name Rainbow stuck with the division. The 42nd arrived in France in November of 1917 and entered the front line in March of 1918; they participated in six major campaigns, remained in almost constant contact with the enemy for 176 days, and made history in the famous battles of Champagne, the Meuse-Argonne, and St.. Mihiel. During the war, one out of sixteen casualties by the American Army was incurred by the 42nd. After World War I was over, the 42nd was officially deactivated in May of 1919.

Two decades passed. When the United States entered into World War II, the 42nd Division was reactivated, with Brigadier General Harry Collins as the Commander. General Collins also said of the Division: "The Rainbow represents the people of our country"; and it was true, as this time the Rainbow Division was made up of men who were chosen from each state of the Union , according to the state's population. In the WWII 42nd Division, the three infantry regiments were numbered 222nd, 232nd, and 242nd. Interestingly, this Rainbow Division would be entering the line not very far from the section of France where World War I Rainbowmen had first entered battle.

General Collins received an early morning phone call from Washington on October 14, 1944, ordering him to stop all other training, and get his three infantry regiments ready to go overseas. They were to spend the next three weeks on squad problems, made very realistic, as they would be using this training very soon. Immediately new combat ranges had been built by engineers, and combat teams worked around the clock packing the equipment for the infantrymen. Orientation films were shown continuously, as well as lectures on avoiding trench-foot and controlling malaria. These men must be informed and prepared for the task that lay ahead of them, and General Collins pushed as hard as he could to make them ready.

Now, in the autumn of 1944, the three infantry regiments of the 42nd Rainbow Division were being rushed overseas, ahead of the other units of their division.

According to the Combat History of the 42nd, the men of the regiments were restricted to Camp Gruber on November 11. Outfitted in their   new fatigues, they slept on the floor after all the beds were removed and checked into the camp supply office. Relatives who lived close enough to make the trip went out to the camp to have a last bit of time with their sons, husbands, or sweethearts; soldiers with families far away wrote letters home assuring their loved ones that they would soon return. Berlie's sister Beatrice and her husband Roy visited him before he left Camp Gruber.

On November 13 the troops began marching onto the train of Pullmans and troop-sleepers, as the Rainbow Division band played "The Rainbow Song". The farewells had been said, the waiting was over, and the 42nd Infantry was on its way to war. Even though they had not yet officially been told their destination, most of the men were aware that they were on their way to Camp Kilmer, New Jersey, which meant Europe. Camp Kilmer, 32 miles from New York, was the largest staging area in the United States, and soldiers were housed there till they embarked on the ships that carried them across the ocean.

Once the trains began rolling eastward, the soldiers, relieved that their good-byes were over, settled down for the long ride. Some caught up on lost sleep, while others kept card games going or argued over war issues, and training and instruction continued onboard as the train moved along. When they arrived at Camp Kilmer and marched off the trains, they were processed, given medical Inspections and shots, and checks of clothing and equipment. With the long lines, they had time on their hands to write letters home, these letters being the first to be censored for security reasons. Many took a 12-hour pass to New York before their shipping orders came. Then on the 25th of November, the three regiments, with a headquarters detachment led by Brigadier

General Henning Linden, marched aboard the waiting ship at Pier 6 in New York and began the ocean voyage to Europe. Twelve days had passed since they had boarded the trains in Oklahoma; twelve days to think about where they were headed, and very few had any real idea of what war looked like or felt like up close. Some of these men had never been on any kind of boat at all; but all four thousand of them were in for a ride they would never forget. As the USS General William Black pulled away from Pier 6 and out into the Atlantic Ocean, the soldiers watched the Statue of Liberty slowly disappearing from view; and not yet having found their sea-legs, they began realizing the meaning of the word "seasick". Private Berlie Forehand was no exception.

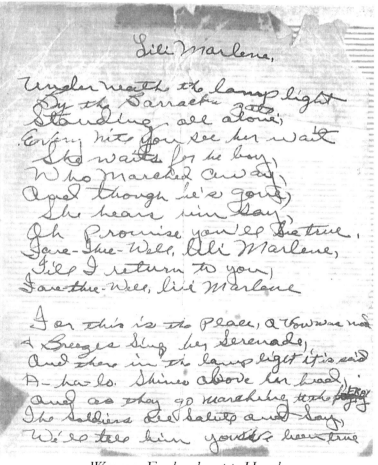

War song Forehand sent to Hazel.

CHAPTER SIX

Crossing the Atlantic

A few days after the ship left New York Harbor and was well out to sea, Forehand plunked down on his bunk, took out his pen and paper and began a letter home. Some of the other guys were writing letters as he was, others just lying on their backs staring at the low ceiling overhead, lost in thought, and one soldier was entertaining them all with familiar songs on his accordion, music that brought memories of home and loved ones to mind. As he played the western tune "Don't Fence Me In", Forehand realized how much he already missed his family, and that even though he was certainly not alone on this crowded ship, he was lonesome.

November 30, '44

At Sea

Dearest Sweethearts,

Wonder how my sweet little family is tonite? Fine I hope, as for me I'm all ok. We're all lying around in our compartment listening to one of our boys play the accordion, he's really good at it too. Makes me think of you all and home, it's really hard to be so far away, and each time the ship rocks, which is just as regular as a clock, it puts me still farther, but the day is coming, and its not too long off, when I'll ride the waves headed HOME. Darling I dreamed last night that we went someplace new to us, we were very happy. Just what we want,uh, honey? Tell Peggy and Janice to be sweet and pray for Dada, I'm coming to play with them some day. Well, Sweetheart, I'll close, so be good to yourself and our sweet babies. Write often, I need your letters and your prayers.

Forever yours, Dada

Two days later and four time zones away, Forehand and the other soldiers in his quarters lay in their bunks listening to the radio broadcast of the Army and Navy football game, an exciting diversion to the constant rolling of the ship. He had helped build big ships like this one back on his job at the shipyard, but it sure was a different thing to be crossing the ocean on one, and never getting used to the back and forth motion that brought on the nausea . He didn't get to write Hazel yesterday, so he reached for his pen and started writing.

December 2, 1944

At Sea

"Dearest Wife and Babies:

Hope you all are getting along fine, as for me, I've been seasick all day and believe you me, it's a terrible condition to be in. I'll sure be glad when I can get some sand or mud between my toes. I didn't write you last night, I felt ok but I was sleepy. So I lay down at 7 and couldn't get to sleep till 11. You know how I always prop my knees up in the air? Well, I can't do it here, the rock of the ship keeps me rolling too much. Well Honey, it's five o'clock here and one back home. I'm lying in bunk listening to Army and Navy football game. Hazel, hon, here's another suggestion for the boy's name, Jerome. Sure hope you get along good, don't you and babies stay at home by yourselves at nite, stay with your Mama and spend some nites with (my) Mama too. Our time on ship is 2/3 gone, I'll sure be glad when the other 1/3 is up, I've never been so sick and tired of anything in all my days. I'll close now, so you and babies be sweet. Write often.

Lovingly yours, Dada

Time onboard ship passed slowly; sometimes it seemed as if one day ran into another. Forehand looked forward to mealtimes, then hoped he could keep down what he had just eaten. "It sure will be good to get back on solid ground again" was a constant thought, not only to Forehand; similar comments could be heard from most of these young soldiers unaccustomed to the rolling motion of the sea. The ship zigzagged through the ocean in an effort to avoid enemy mines and submarines, making the crossing days longer than it would normally take. Sometimes it seemed they would never reach land; and even though they were given assigned duties daily, training and receiving instructions, they still could only imagine what it would be like when they finally arrived. Their only consolation was that this crossing couldn't take forever, and each day brought them nearer to their landing, and to the war. Forehand wanted to assure his wife of his well-being, so he took the time to write her an encouraging letter before sleep.

December 5, '44
At Sea

Dearest Wife and Babies:
Wonder how you all are getting along tonite. Fine, I hope, as for me I'm all ok, just a bit lonesome. Sure would like to see you all tonite but the ocean almost separates us now. Our day is coming again some sweet day, though, so keep your chin up for Dada, I'll be ok. So don't worry about me, I won't be in combat for a long time yet. Well Honey I sure hope you get along good, and I hope it's a big sweet baby like Peggy and Janice was, take good care of yourself and babies. I'll take the best care of myself I can. Sugar, you can write and ask me any questions and as many as you wish, I'll ans all I can. I'll close for now, so be good and write often.
Your Loving Dada

50

Twelve days out to sea, and farther and farther away from home, Private Forehand sure did want to know how Hazel and the girls were doing, but he knew he would not get mail until they had landed in France. Earlier today he had sat down and made a Christmas V-mail card for her and the girls . . . hopefully it would make it to them before the holidays. A few days earlier he had met a Guardsman on the ship who had worked with him back at the shipyard in Panama City and they had been spending some time together. This time he would see if these letters really went postage-free and so he began a letter . . .

Dec. 6, '44
At Sea

Dearest Wife and Babies:

Wonder how my little family is today. Fine, I hope, this leaves me feeling fine. I sure do wanta hear from you all, guess I will soon if you've been writing. Darling, I fixed you and babies a V-mail Christmas card today, hope you get it. I've been sending all my V-mail by airmail, or putting 6 cent stamps on them. I think they go airmail without the stamp, I'm sending this one free just to find out, let me know, will you? There's a Coast Guard on this ship I used to work with at W.W. yard, lives in Millville, he's going home a few days when he gets back to the U.S. We stay together lots. Sweetheart, don't send my Parker pen, I have a good one "Eversharp". Honey, you can write me anything you want and ask any and as many questions as you desire, I'll ans all I can. Well darling I'll close hoping to hear from you all soon.

Your loving Dada, Berlie

51

Though his letters would not be mailed until the ocean crossing was over, Forehand wrote every two or three days, knowing Hazel would be happy to finally receive news from him. Just the sight of land would make him happy; some days it took all he had just to stand upright and walk when waves of seasickness would come. He thought about how it must be to spend weeks and months on a ship as Navy men did, and figured they just had to get used to it. At least he wasn't the only one in that shape, seemed like a lot of his fellow soldiers were going through the same thing. This ocean crossing was taking longer than was normally the case, having to zigzag around in an effort to avoid areas that might be mined or where enemy ships or U-boats could be on the lookout to fire on them. It might take a few days longer, but it was worth it if it could help ensure their safe arrival, and being seasick was just part of it. At least a foxhole would be solid underneath your feet, thought Private Forehand, as he sat down to write on Wednesday night . . .

> Dearest Wife and Babies:
> I know about how you feel at not hearing from me lately, but you understand, we have been rocking and rolling as many days as our rent was in S.C. I've sure been sick lots but I'm just about straight now. There's surely no pleasure in traveling at sea, I'm dizzy all the time. I think I can live better in a foxhole. Well, Honey, I sure hope and pray you and our precious babies are well, my thoughts are with you all, always. Darling, please don't worry about me, we won't hit combat for six months if ever. I don't think I'll be over here very long, and when I get back to the states I can go home to stay, forever. Honey, if I were you, I'd stay with Granny and Joe till I got in good shape again, but don't put up on her as some have done, pay your way. Well,

Sweetheart, I'll close. Tell babys Dada's ok and is coming home sometime. Write often. May God bless you all for me.

All my love forever, Dada.

As the ship neared its destination, the thoughts of soon setting foot on solid ground overcame his anxiety at what lay ahead. He knew that with every wave, with every roll of this ship, they were getting that much nearer to war; and they would all soon find out just how ready they were for it. These foot soldiers had trained, studied and practiced with the gear and arms they would soon be called on to put into action. And so the ship rolled on in its steady forward motion, and a new kind of anxiety began to pervade the ship, as Forehand and every man like him began to sense more urgency, while at the same time an excitement about finally getting to walk off this rolling hunk of steel.

CHAPTER SEVEN

Command Post 2

The troopship sailed into the Mediterranean Sea and on Saturday, December 9, the long rocky ride was over at last as landing was made in Marseilles, France. Salty air saturated PFC Berlie Forehand's lungs as he greeted this new world for the first time. The thick rolling clouds assumed position, creating a peaceful mural against the crystal blue sky.

Having had time to envision what lay ahead, he noted how this vast portrait that now unfolded before him contradicted the mental picture he had carried with him for this very day, not so unlike the lazy afternoons far away he spent with his beloved What a cruel joke mother nature was playing now, or was it? Was she allowing this scenery so that he and other GIs like him could hang on to one last memory before the storms of war rolled in? "Move it!", the sharp voice that carried orders thundered and brought him quickly back to the dismal arena of port where he could already see the scuffle of soldiers, jeeps, and forklifts preparing to unload the cargo and the mountain of supplies that were needed to outfit all the GI's arriving and those that would follow. Soon the whole port was a sea of olive drab, and blurs of black, moving like ants all around. He took in all the new scenery, trying not to miss one detail, as he planned to write his sweetheart about it, hoping to ease her mind about this dangerous place so far from her and his little girls. How he missed them already, and longed to hold them. "Soon", he whispered silently to himself, trying to block out any thought that he might not, and quickly putting that thought in the back of his mind, he made a promise to himself that he was here on business, to fight, to win, and to return to them.

A thin layer of water coated the rail and soaked his hands that were slowly growing numb in the stinging air swirling in off of the water. The steel deck of the ship only added to that misery, yielding a grim reminder all too real to the young GI's: this was war, and they were in it. It was that simple, and no matter how far they tried to place it in the back of their minds, they couldn't escape it. Many had tried onboard ship, playing cards, dominoes, singing; they had even managed to get in on the Army-Navy football game while out at sea. But when night had fallen and each was alone in his bedroll, his mind raced: what was in store for him? Would he see those he loved so much again? Would his death come quickly, or would he just be invalid for the rest of his life? These fears were real and each GI had to deal with them in his own way or become a victim to them. He was infantry and he knew it; it all came down to him and the men like him. Gerries didn't just walk up and surrender to the planes or the ships. They had to be beaten, and that was what he had trained for so long and so hard for. The only thing left was combat, and the only question in his mind was, was he ready?

Soon he was walking down the ramp into this sea of green he had seen from on deck, and it struck him how strange it was hearing the French spoken by the old Frenchmen working on the docks. With all the movement of men and vehicles it was noisy. He hadn't noticed till now, being so absorbed in everything that was going through his mind, all the while trying to remember all that was said when they were being given orders on all that would follow…where to go, who was in charge, what came when; so he just stayed focused on the olive canvas in front of him and kept moving.

The familiar scent of diesel filled the air now as forklifts, trucks, and other vehicles raced by on their way to drop off supplies or pick up officers, whatever the need was. Soon he found himself marching up a road with the rest of the men. What had been solid ground now turned into rocky, rut-laden earth and mud, and his legs soon began to burn as the steep grade of the road took its toll on the men burdened with supplies and personal belongings as they made their way to the command post and awaited orders. This rocky, windswept piece of ground was known as Command Post 2 or simply CP2.

The bitter wind stung his face as the sweat slowly turned to misery. The temperature must have been near freezing, and he blew into his hands to try and fight off the cold. Some men around him lit up cigarettes and chatted as they waited, and before long he found himself setting up a pup tent and situating his belongings. Chow time must be soon, he thought, as his stomach was letting him know. After trying to keep down the meals served on the rolling ship, it would almost be a

new experience to eat without losing it, now that the ground was solid under his feet again. And as far as the cold, he would just have to get used to it, there were many more miserable freezing days ahead for him and for all these foot soldiers.

After a nice hot meal, especially good considering the cold wind that blew in off the water, it was time to set the camp in order. By the time darkness fell, PFC Forehand and all the other newly arrived troops had begun to realize how very close war now seemed to be. At night there was blackout; after all, such a huge encampment all lighted up would make a fine target for the German plane which occasionally flew overhead, with anti-aircraft guns barking at it. As he crawled into his bedroll in his pup tent, he didn't miss at all the rolling motion of the ship that had brought him to this distant shore, and sleep came quickly.

Morning came early, and the bustle of thousands of GI's beginning their day brought a feeling very different from basic training or the voyage over. Now that war was a reality to these GI's, they put a more intense effort into the continuous training, realizing more than ever the importance of each detail. They knew they would soon be pushing forward into territory they were not really familiar with, they had better pay attention, learn all they could, as it could save their own lives. Phrases such as: "Get trained, not killed", and "Train now for victory", "Trained fighters last longer", and "Trained soldiers win wars" were repeated often enough that they became part of the mind-set of these soldiers. They were also taught not to let rumors affect their actions, hearing: "It's a pretty empty mind that's so hard up it has to take in rumors", and "anytime you hear one of those latrine rumors, remember its source", and "Stop rumors, don't start them". They were told that in combat they would do exactly what they were taught to do in training, so it must become an automatic thing to do things the right way. Training was intense, it had to be.

The troops were reminded that their letters home would be censored, and officers must make sure that no one even inadvertently put any information in their letters that would jeopardize security, whereabouts, or plans. Back stateside, posters warning "Loose lips sink ships" and "Less said, less dead" were plastered in public view to remind people to be careful what they wrote and what they said. "This is war, and anything that you write in a letter that could be read by the enemy or passed on to the enemy, giving away our whereabouts or plans, could mean we lose men, even lose battles; we are not here to lose men, or to lose battles, we are here to fight this war and win it with as few casualties as possible"—words like these spoken by the officers in charge echoed in PFC Forehand's mind as he sat down and simply wrote above the date of his next letter,

> Tuesday, December 12
> Southern France
>
> Dearest Wife and Babies:
> I will try and ans your two sweet and welcome letters I rec'd last nite. Hope you all are still ok, as for me I'm all okay except for a cold. I have a hard time keeping my nose clean. Honey, I've dreamed of you and our sweet babies for the last three nites. I can't help but worry about you all. I also dreamed the baby was born and he was a big nice boy. I sure hope you all are well and getting along good. Sweetheart, please don't worry about me. I'm in a perfectly safe place, the weather is pretty cold but we were prepared for cold weather before we left the states. We sleep under our pup tents but we have a bedroll to sleep in, and believe it or not, I'd rather stay right here for the next four months than to take basic over again, unless I could have you all with me, as we were at Croft. I sleep good twelve hours every nite. So you see, I'm getting along fine and there is no need of you worrying about me, Honey.

59

The country over here is beautiful, nothing like I had expected. There's plenty of wine and women over here, but you know me, NO wine and women for me, I'm here on a business trip, I came over to fight, nothing more. I sure hope the cake you sent me comes on to me, we have plenty to eat, but some of your good cakes would sure be appreciated. If you wish, you may send one every few weeks. Well, Sweethearts, I'll close, so write often, you and the babies be sweet, and pray for Dada.

Your loving husband and Dada, Berlie Forehand

PFC Forehand leaned back and stretched, thinking of his wife and children, hoping they were alright. Today he would look around and maybe he'd run across more of the men he had been with in basic at Camp Croft; some of them had become almost like family in the sixteen weeks they had spent together, and it was good to see familiar faces and hear familiar voices. He had heard they were here somewhere on CP2, and he intended to find them if he could. He had a little time before he had to show up for several more hours of training, so he put away his pen, buttoned up his heavy jacket and took off at a brisk pace to see who he could find. Maybe the walk would warm him up some, at least. Gusts of freezing wind caused him to speed up; he sure hoped he could find his buddies, he thought, as he pulled out a handkerchief and blew his nose once again.

That evening after mail call, just before bedtime, he sat down with the letter he had just received and read quickly through it. "Still no news of the baby", he thought, but he was relieved that all seemed to be well back home. It was too late to write tonight, but in the morning he would write her about how he had found his Croft buddies today; he smiled remembering how surprised they had been when he walked right up to them this morning. As he snuggled into his bedroll, the last thing he thought about as he drifted off to sleep was his dark-haired, brown-eyed sweetheart and their two little tow-headed girls. He sure did miss them.

When he awoke early the next morning, it was just as cold, if not colder, than it had been the night before. He pulled on his boots, thinking how good a cup of hot coffee would taste, and after a quick trip to the latrine, he joined up with his buddies and headed to the mess tent. After a couple cups of the steaming coffee he had woke up thinking about, and some good hot chow, he had a few minutes to get back to the pup tent and take out his pen and sheet of paper. He had heard the news that in the next few days they would be leaving CP2, and he didn't know how easy it would be to write a letter once they were on the move. And he was still happy about having found his Camp Croft buddies yesterday and wanted to tell Hazel about it; she would remember them, as she had spent those four months with him while he was in basic, and she had met some of them. And just writing a letter made him feel a little closer, seeing their faces in his mind as he wrote the words that would reassure them of his safety.

Dec. 13, 1944

Dearest Ones:

I will try and ans your sweet and welcome letter I rec'd last nite, sure was glad to hear from you all, this leaves me getting along just fine, hope you all are well and getting along good. Honey, remember Chastain the guitar picker, Hoch, and Hinnant? They're all over here with me, most all the boys from Croft are over here now, I've seen most of them, I heard they were here so I looked them up. Boy they were sure surprised. Sweetheart, I'd sure love to see you, Peggy and Jan Von, tell them Dada is all okay, I'm always thinking of you all, I'll be with you again some day (I pray). Honey, I've not got my cake yet, I'm still hoping for it. I guess we'll have a new baby

when you get this, then I'll have a family of four
waiting for me. I can't be with you all while you're
sick but my thoughts and prayers will be. Well
Sweethearts, news is out and so is space, so I'll close.
You all be good, take care of yourself and our sweet
babies. Write often.
    Your loving husband and Dada, Berlie
P.S. tell Granny, Joe, and all hello.

That night Forehand had guard duty, and even all bundled up in
the warm wool uniform and heavy jacket they had all been issued, the
bitter cold bit through the fabric as he stood at his post shivering, and
he realized this thing had just begun, there would be a lot more cold
nights ahead. At least there was plenty of time to think when most of
the camp was quiet and still in the pitch blackness of night.

When his hours of guard duty were over, Forehand quietly made
his way to his pup tent and fell into his bedroll for a few hours sleep.
After a schedule of being on two and off four, another day came to an
end and he finally had time to sit down and get another letter written.
Suddenly feeling lonely for Hazel and the girls, he picked up the picture
of the four of them, the one they had gone to the studio to have made
on the day he had enlisted and bought his first uniform, studied it
closely and longingly for a minute or two, then began a letter.

Dec. 14, 1944

My Dearest Wife and babies,
I'll try and answer your sweet letter of Nov. 29th
which I received yesterday, glad you all were well
and hope you continue to be okay. This leaves me
all ok except for the cold I've had for the last few
days and guess I'll keep it all winter, but my
tonsils haven't bothered me any as yet. Honey, I
wanted to write you and get it off today, but I was

on guard last night, and today I was on two and off four, but I didn't have time to write. We had no mail call today so I didn't hear from you all today. Sweetheart, I'm writing this sitting in my pup tent by the light of a kerosene flambo I fixed up just for the purpose of writing, it also helps to warm up my tent. It's pretty cold here now, we have a hard winter ahead of us, but we'll make it fine. You should see the clothes we have, we're equipped with the best and we have plenty of it, too. So don't worry about me being out in the cold, if I'm cold it will probably be my fault, and when you are sitting in by a good warm fire, don't feel sorry for your little dada for being out in the cold, instead just feel proud you got a man that can take it. Darling, I'd sure like to see you and my sweet babies tonite, but instead I'm sitting here lonely, just looking at the picture of us four and praying for the day when we can all be together again. Well honey, I'll close for now, so goodnight, sweet dreams, and may God bless you all for me, Write often.

All my love forever, Dada

His letter finished, Forehand extinguished the flambo and crawled into his sack, thankful for the thick warm bedroll on this frosty night, and feeling a little anxious knowing they would shortly be dismantling these pup tents and heading north. "Better get on to sleep", he thought, realizing that once they were moving, it might not be as easy to do so.

Forehand decided it might be a good idea to number the letters he wrote home, so it would be easy to tell if all the letters arrived. A day and a half later, he sat down to write, having been thinking of his

oldest little girl, Peggy. Today was her fourth birthday, and he sure would love to be home celebrating her birthday, watching her blow out the candles on her cake, singing to her as he played his guitar. But he was far away and all he could do was think about it, maybe he would be there for her birthday next year. Well, at least he had eaten a piece of cake last night when he went into the nearby town with some of the other guys and went to the Red Cross club for American servicemen— it was a nice break from the routine and starkness of camp, anyway. In a day or two they would be packing up and moving out, so a pass into town was a treat they may not get for a while. It was sometimes hard to think of news to write about; at least this time he had something a bit more interesting to tell. He sat down and began a letter.

> #1 December 16, 1944
> Southern France
>
> Dearest Sweethearts:
> Just a few lines to let you all hear from me. This leaves me getting long just fine, surely hope you all are ok. Well honey, today is Dada's grown daughter's birthday. I'd give anything to be there with her, Jan Von and you. Maybe I'll be there for her 5th birthday and possibly for your 24th birthday, hope so anyway Darling, I went to town last nite, or yesterday afternoon, some town, too. The more I see over here, the more thankful I am that I'm an American. I went to the Red Cross Club for American servicemen, and had coffee and cake. I was offered 750 francs (equal to $15.00) for $6.00 American dollars, guess it's because our money will always be good and their francs won't, but I still have my 6 bucks. Can't tell you name of town but you can guess, can't you? Honey, guess you're

still wondering what was cut off my letter back in U.S.A. Well, I was telling you I wasn't gonna write any more for a while, but for you not to worry. Guess it was a bit too plain, so it was cut off. I've not rec'd my cake yet. Well, Sweet, I've no news, so I'll close, answer soon.

Your Loving husband and Dada, Berlie

On that very day, December 16, the Germans launched a massive counter-offensive in the Ardennes. American forces were being pushed back, creating a "bulge" in the line, and the U.S. Third Army was moving north to cut off Germany's attack, which left a gap in the line that the Seventh Army was being forced to stretch out and fill until more forces arrived. This would become the largest land battle of World War II in which the United States participated; more than a million men would fight in this battle—it was Hitler's last-ditch attempt to bring Germany back into winning the war—this Battle of the Bulge.

Although the Rainbow Infantrymen knew they were on the verge of leaving CP2, Forehand, and likely many others as well, wrote a letter home on the 17th that showed no indication of moving out. He had a lot on his mind, but not much of it could be put into a letter. He figured a short letter was better than no letter at all, especially if you didn't know when you'd get a chance to write again; it could be a while, he thought. He could tell her about seeing a few more of his Croft buddies that day, and that he missed her and the girls So he sat down and penned a few lines.

#2 December 17, 1944
Southern France

Dearest Wife and Babies:
Just a few lines to say hello, hope you 3 "or" 4 are well and enjoying life, as for me, I'm all ok. I seen Hoch

and several other boys I was in basic with last nite, they were sure surprised to see me. Darling, I try to write to you all every day, but I know my letters are dull, as I can't write of anything but myself. But I guess you're glad to get letters from me even though they're dull. I'm sorry about Belle having trouble with her leg, hope she's better now. I'd sure love to see you and babies, I'm always thinking of you all. Well, Sweetheart, I'll close, so write often and don't worry about me,

　　　　Your loving Husband and Dada, Berlie

On that day, December 17, the second day of the German offensive—the Battle of the Bulge—German forces intercepted and captured a large group of U.S. artillerymen driving south with the 7th Armored Division. Of the 140 men taken prisoner, 86 were shot, simply herded into a meadow and gunned down—others escaped and managed to survive this massacre at Malmedy. Another American force discovered the snow-covered bodies of the soldiers that same day, and when they found out from survivors what had happened, the story spread quickly throughout the American divisions, causing the Americans to fight harder and with more determination. It also showed the Allied Command that they were up against a full-scale German offensive and led them to make some important decisions in which armies were repositioned and maneuvers changed.

The GI's of the 42nd Rainbow Division were as ready as they would ever be for action; from basic to shipboard to CP2, they had been trained for battle. Every infantryman knew his weapons, his tactics, his skills, and what was expected of him. Their officers had done everything they knew to do to prepare them for war. They could not forget the words of Division Commander Maj. Gen. Collins: "You will never, in the long nights after the war, hear the soul of some boy cry out that you were careless in teaching him". In the First

World War, the Rainbow Division had earned fame as one of the U.S. Army's hardest fighting divisions, and Maj. Gen. Collins felt heavily the responsibility of making sure that the honor and respect they had gained would be maintained by this reactivated Rainbow Division; he would do all he could, in fact, to help them make the Rainbowmen of World War I proud. His words demonstrated his thoughts once again when he said: "We are determined to learn it (the job of a soldier) so that every man who ever wore the Rainbow may look upon his old emblem with a new delight, with a vision dimmed by nothing more than his own tears of reawakened pride".

CHAPTER EIGHT

Moving Out

On December 18, Command Post 2 was crawling with equipment and vehicles; pup tents were dismantled and folded, and personal belongings were packed for the road. Forehand took another look at his family's photo before he rolled up the frame in some clothes and stuffed it into his bag. He and the thousands of other infantrymen there had been waiting for these moving orders for several days; now it was time. They had been assigned to the Third Army and were being sent to help fight in the Battle of the Bulge. When all was ready for them to leave CP2, they climbed aboard 40 and 8 boxcars (built to hold 40 men or 8 horses) and the train began the drive northward. But along the way their orders were changed, and Task Force Linden— as the three 42nd Rainbow Infantry Division regiments were now known as—was reassigned; now they would be a component of the Seventh Army and were being sent to relieve elements of the 36th Infantry Division, from Texas, in the area of Strasbourg. The move took several days, and along the way, Forehand wrote another letter with a positive tone, thinking of how near it was to Christmas and how he would miss being with his family for the holidays. "Maybe I'll be home before next Christmas", he thought as he wrote letter . . .

#3 France
Dec. 21, 1944

Hello Sweethearts!
Wonder how you all are getting along this cold cloudy day? Fine I hope, as for me I'm getting along just fine. Well, Honey, it's only four days till Christmas. I'd sure love to be with you and babies, but I'll spend this one a long ways from you all, but Christmas will always be once a year back home, and I think I'll be with you all next one, and every one thereafter. I'll be thinking of you all Christmas. Darling, my fruit cake hasn't got to me yet, I'm still looking for it though, but maybe you

didn't have it wrapped sufficient to come over seas.
Honey, don't expect too many letters from me now,
we don't send out mail but about every two or three
days. I'll try to write every other day or as often as
possible, you write to me as often as you can, news
from you and the sweet babies mean very much to
me. Well, Honey, I'll close, so don't worry over me,
I'm ok. Give my love to the babies and write often.
　　　　　Your loving Dada, Berlie

Task Force Linden continued on their way to Strasbourg, still
a couple days away for the lengthy convoy. The French countryside
was beautiful, though different from the countryside back home in
northwest Florida. Private Forehand made comparisons in his mind
as they passed by little French towns, and when he got a chance later
that evening, he wrote Hazel about it. And since he wasn't getting to
write anyone else as often as he wrote to her, he asked her to let his
Mama know that he was alright and would write to her when he could.
He didn't want anyone back home to be worrying about him; God
willing, he would be seeing them all again, at least that was his hope.
The farther north this convoy got, the lower the temperature fell. Only
three days till Christmas, and it just might be his first white Christmas,
at least it was sure cold enough to snow.

　　　　　　　　　　　#4 December 22, 1944
　　　　　　　　　　　　　　France

Dearest Wife and Babies,
I'll try and write you all a few lines, surely hope
you all are getting along good, I'm all ok and safe
myself. I had a pleasant dream of you all last nite.
Honey, let Mama know each time you hear from
me, tell her not to worry about me, I'll be all ok and
write to all of them as often as I can. Sweetheart,

I've seen quite a bit of France, some parts of it are really beautiful. People sure live different over here, too. Every family lives in a town, with their house and barn in the same building, no buildings are made of wood. I sure do want to see you and our sweet babies. This thing will be over, over here some day, and it may not be too long, then we'll be going back to our loved ones to stay. Well Sweethearts, don't worry about me, write often, take care of you four for me.

Your loving Dada, Berlie

The next day, December 23, the Rainbow Infantry Division arrived near Strasbourg and, rather than set up pup tents, they were billeted in school houses and old forts. They had running water, which at that point seemed like a real luxury, and they would sleep warmer inside a real building. The GI's almost cheerfully unloaded supplies and their belongings and settled down for the night. It sure felt good to be inside, away from the freezing weather, even if it was just for one night, thought Private Forehand as he stretched out, closed his eyes and quickly fell asleep.

In the morning, Forehand sat down to write Hazel and the girls again, hoping they were enjoying a good Christmas. It was Christmas Eve, and he imagined they were spending it with Granny Belle and the others, eating Christmas cookies and playing with their cousins. He hadn't received any letters for more than a week; they had been on the move so mail hadn't caught up with them yet. He sure would love to be watching the girls open their Christmas gifts; and he still didn't know if there was a new baby in the little wooden house in Kinard. He had heard that holidays away from your family were the hardest times; now he understood the truth in that.

5 December 24, 1944
France

Hello Sweethearts,

How's my sweet little family getting along now days? Sure hope you all are well and having a nice Christmas. I can just picture the ladies having lots of fun with their teddy bear and other things Ole Santa sent them. I'd sure love to be there with you all. Honey, it's really cold over here, but I'm getting along just swell, I don't know where or what I'll be doing tomorrow, but today I'm in a big nice room by a hot heater, enjoying life as much as any one over here can. I don't intend to be cold as long as clothes will keep me warm, I've got plenty and I'll wear all of it I can get around me if I need that to stay warm, so don't worry about me. Darling, I haven't rec'd my fruitcake or my gloves yet, I need the gloves, too. The cake would be good, too. I haven't had any mail in 9 days, been moving around quite a lot, maybe I'll get lots of mail in a day or so. Well, Darling, I'll close, you all be sweet. Write to Dada often.

Worlds of love, Dada— BF

On Christmas Eve and Christmas Day, the three infantry regiments of the Rainbow moved into defensive positions on the front line—a 19-mile front— along the Rhine River, and were placed under control of the 79th Division. Forehand's regiment, the 242nd, was situated on the south of the city of Strasbourg, with the 222nd in the city and the 232nd north of the city. The Germans were across the river, also on the defensive. When they fired a few bursts of automatic weapons fire into the Rainbow positions and an entire company returned fire, the Germans stopped firing. They weren't sure now what new unit was there firing at them, and when a couple of German patrol boats trying to cross the river were spotted by the Rainbow, who opened fire with machine guns on them, they turned their boats around and made for the other side. Forehand was on guard all Christmas Day, and when he was relieved at 8 o'clock that evening, he found that Uncle Sam had not forgotten it was Christmas and had a tasty turkey dinner with the trimmings prepared for the GI's that evening. The officers served tables, a human touch not unnoticed by the young GI's. The hot feast was even more welcome after being on guard out in the cold all day, and it kind of made up for being so far away from home and family on Christmas. After enjoying the turkey dinner and comradeship of the other GI's for a while around the table, Forehand wrote a letter to his ladies to tell them about how he spent this Christmas Day.

#6 Christmas Day 1944
"Somewhere in France"

Dearest Wife and Babies,

Well, here I am again, and I'm feeling fine, too, surely hope you all are ok. Honey, it's 9 o'clock now. I've just finished eating a big supper, I was on guard all day, came in at 8, and boy we sure had a good supper too. Plenty of good turkey, with everything that goes with it, and we really did enjoy sitting down to a table to plenty of good eats, too. Uncle Sam really sees to it that the soldiers have a good dinner on holidays. I've thought of you and babies all day, wondering if you are sick. Sweetheart, if you knew how good I'm getting along and how safe I am here, you wouldn't worry about me. It's not as hard as basic was, the weather is cold, but I've plenty of clothes to stay warm. Honey, our officers waited on the table for us GI's at supper. Every man in the outfit is good men. Well, Sweet, I'm sleepy, so I'll close. Ans soon.

Your loving Dada, Berlie

The following day a lot of troop movement began, and would continue for the next week and a half. With a fierce battle being waged in the Bulge up north, units were being moved to fill in gaps in the line left by other units being sent north. The Seventh Army line was spreading out thinner, so plans began forming to withdraw from Strasbourg into the Vosges mountains in order to shorten the lines. Troop movement plans changed and then changed again, as the French decided they wanted to hold the city of Strasbourg and the American troops would hold the line along the Rhine River. They would not give any ground back to the Germans but make them fight for it. Forehand's regiment was moved several times in the next few days, as were the other two infantry regiments. With all the moving around, mail took longer to find them, as Forehand wrote in letter a couple of days later . . .

#7 December 27, 1944
France

Sweetheart,

I haven't rec'd a letter from you for the past two weeks, but we're looking for some mail any day now. We will be glad to hear from you all, too. You all should hear from me pretty often, as I write you most every day. Well, honey, I guess you and all the folks are listening to the news from over here and worrying lots about me when I'm faring better than I did in basic. I'm sleeping in a good warm house every nite. I'm on guard duty 8 hours a day, getting plenty of good eats, so why worry about me? Darling, when a $5.00 c.o.d. package comes, take it out, it's a book of my outfit.

Write to Dada often.

Your loving Dada, BF

As they moved through France, the GI's were often sheltered by the local people, who realized these American GI's were in their country to fight for them. The least they could do in return was offer a warm room, even a hot bowl of soup or piece of cake to the friendly GI's. Forehand was staying in the home of a French family, enjoying their warm fire, when he wrote letter . . .

#8, December 29, '44
France

Dearest Wife and Babies:
Here I am again, hoping you all are well and getting along fine, this leaves me ok, and I'm feeling just fine, too. Darling, it's been 16 days since I heard from you all, or anyone, guess I'll get lots of mail, tho, once it catches up. I'm sitting in a nice warm room while writing this, the people are nice to us. I can't talk to them, but I can let them know I wanta sit by their fire and write, they sound like babies trying to talk. Guess I sound the same to them. There's a baby here about the size of Janice, I gave her chewing gum, she sure likes it. Honey, I dream of you most every nite, the happiest moment of my life is still to come, seeing you all again. Write often.
Dada

Only a soldier far away from home and family, and fighting in a war that he hoped to come out of alive and whole, could understand how getting letters from home could make his day and give him something to think about. A few minutes of reading the news from loved ones provided a momentary distraction from this business of war and a reminder that folks back home cared about what was happening to him. Even news of the most routine things, the family dog having puppies, the baby cutting a new tooth, how Grandma and Grandpa were getting along, things happening in their hometown, kept the GI connected to things back home and lifted his morale.

Private Forehand had been counting the days since he had gotten any mail, but he and the other GI's in his company figured it had to catch up with them sooner or later. He had been thinking a lot about moving away from Kinard and going to a new place when he got home from this war, so he decided to share his plans with Hazel when he sat down to write the next letter.

#9, December 30, 1944
France

Dearest Sweethearts,

Wonder how you all are today? Surely hope you all are well and enjoying life, as for myself, I'm getting along just fine. I haven't weighed since I've been over here, but I do believe I'm fattening, and I feel good all the time. Well, Darling, it's been 17 days since I had a letter from you all, it was written 29th Nov., so I don't know how you all have been getting along for the past 32 days, but I'm most sure we have a new baby by now, hope it's as big and sweet as our two sweet ladies. Honey, when I come home, if my health and body is in good condition, I'm gonna build us a new house, farther south, I already have it all planned out. It's gonna be a low type two story house, with things that are needed for us to live in comfort. I want a small farm, lots of cattle and hogs, and a good saddle barn. Well, sweethearts, it's time for chow, then six hours guard duty. I'll say again, don't worry over me, I'm safe and okay. I'll close, be sweet and write to dada often, kiss the babies for me.

Your loving Dada, Berlie F.

The next morning Forehand went rabbit hunting, as there was snow on the ground and it should be easier to spot a rabbit. He had learned to hunt back home with his big brothers, and it was a nice change of pace for a little while at least. He had always loved being out in the woods, and was completely comfortable with the trees and undergrowth, even with the small animals that made their homes in the boughs and burrows. Only thing different was that back home he never had been concerned about an enemy being out there somewhere with a bead on him. He didn't see any rabbits but enjoyed the walk through the snow-covered woods.

The mail finally was delivered and it made a lot of GI's happy. Mail call was announced and Private Forehand was smiling as he took his handful of letters and walked back to a warmer place to sit down and enjoy reading all of it. "Better enjoy your mail," quipped a GI, "We won't be getting any more till next year." It was New Year's Eve, 1944.

He opened the letters and cards with his pocketknife, and began reading the news from home, saving his copy of the Liberator for last. "Still no news about a new baby in the house,"he said to himself after skimming quickly over all the letters; then he read them all again, more slowly this time so he wouldn't miss anything. His Christmas cards were a week late, but it didn't matter; he read each one a couple times and enjoyed them as much as if they had arrived on time. Having read all eight of the letters and cards, he pulled out his pen and paper and began a letter; he had to let Hazel know her mail had finally found him . . .

#10, December 31, 1944

Dearest Wife and Babies:

I'll try and ans your sweet letters I've just finished reading, the last one being written Dec. 6th. I got 3 letters, 4 Christmas cards from you all, a Christmas card from Papa, and a Liberator, we sure were glad to have mail call again. Honey, I'm sorry you and the babies were sick, hope you all are well by now, this leaves me getting fatter every day. Maybe I'll get my cake soon, I had good cake for dinner, but nothing like yours. Darling, if you haven't already had car fixed, don't let anyone tell you the car needs rings, it don't. The cards you and Peg and Jan sent me were very sweet. It's pretty cold over here. I went rabbit hunting in the snow this morning. Well, Dear, guess I'll close so you all be good and write often, tell my sweet babies I'm coming home some time.

Worlds of love, Dada

CHAPTER NINE

Strasbourg

On the first day of 1945, Hitler, planning to eliminate Allied air power, sent German fighter planes to bombard Allied airfields in Belgium, Holland, and Northern France. In two hours of bombing, 200 planes and many bases were destroyed, but Germany had also suffered great losses, over 300 planes and 253 trained pilots.

On the same day, Forehand's regiment, the 242nd, was moved into Task Force reserve near Holtzheim and Hangenbeiten, tiny snow-covered farm villages only four miles away from Strasbourg, prepared to block a possible enemy attack from the south. They only stayed one night there, moved back the next day to the Vosges mountain line, then moved again two more times in the next day or two. It was New Year's Day, and after enjoying a nice turkey dinner furnished the GI's by Uncle Sam, Forehand wanted to tell Hazel he was doing alright, so he found a seat beside a heater and wrote another letter home. He could hear the sound of children playing on their sleighs outside in the snow, and it kept bringing his own little girls to his mind; he thought again of how he planned to build them a new home—when he made it back home.

#11, January 2, 1945
Somewhere in France

Dearest Sweethearts:

Just a few lines to let you all hear from me. I'm feeling fine, surely hope you four are getting along good. I had my New Year's dinner today, about an hour ago, plenty of turkey and boy it sure was good, too. We moved last night, so we just waited till today to have our turkey. We are still living in houses, I'm sitting by a hot heater now, it's plenty cold outside, the kids are out in the streets with their sleighs and having a time on them, in the frozen snow. Honey, I'd sure love to see you and our sweet babies. I haven't done anything today but think of

you all and how happy we will be when I get back
home with you all. I don't look forward to nothing
but living with you all and building us a good new
home, just like we want. I believe I'll be home before
many months. Well, Sweetheart, guess I'll close.
Kiss all my sweet babies for me. Write often.
Lovingly, your Dada, BF

The winter of '44-'45 was one of the worst on record in Europe,
with ice, snow, and frozen mud adding to the normal difficulties of
war. It was bitterly cold on January 3, and the icy roads were full of
refugees leaving Strasbourg because they thought the American forces
were going to abandon the city to the Germans; so they were trying to
get away and flee back into the part of France that had already been
liberated. Late that afternoon and into the middle of the night the
242nd moved into Brumath, and the first and third battalions moved
on toward the north to relieve the 314th Infantry of the 79th Division
in the line, leaving the Second Battalion in Strasbourg until the vehicles
could return for them. Even with all the moving going on, somehow
the mail arrived and Forehand was happy to receive three letters from
Hazel. In one of her letters she told him that a GI they both know had
been sent home because of battle trauma, which made her wonder if
her Berlie is really doing as well as he says he is in his letters. She was
also wondering if he might run across her brother Leroy who was also
fighting somewhere in France. He found the time to write her a letter
in return, to answer some of her questions, and just to reassure her
that he is alright.

#13, January 4, 1945
France

Hello Sweethearts:
Here I come in answer to three sweet letters I rec'd
last nite, of Dec. 13-15 & 18, sure was glad to hear

from you. This leaves me getting along fine, surely hope you all are ok. Darling, I'm sorry you stay so lonesome and worry so much, you really shouldn't think so much about me being away, just let every day come and go. I'll be with you all some day. I don't worry about you and our sweet babies, I know you'll take good care of them and yourself. I should know whether it's a son or a girl soon. I don't wonder at (name omitted) being crazy, it's plenty to drive any man crazy. I think it's a good distance to where Leroy is, I'd like to see him. Darling, start writing airmail, and send me a V-mail ready addressed in every letter. Tell the ladies Dada said be sweet, and to pray for Dada. Tell all the folks hello, and write often.

Worlds of love, Dada

The following day, January 5, was a day that was not to be forgotten in the history of the 42nd Rainbow Division. The First French Army was moving in to take over the city of Strasbourg, while the American forces held the line along the Rhine River. The Germans crossed the Rhine north of the city during the predawn hours and after daylight launched an attack on four towns in the vicinity. The Rainbow Division, though stretched thinly across the front, and against stronger equipment and weapons, came against heavy enemy fire but refused to be stopped, even with hot shells bursting all around them. They pressed forward, and although they sustained heavy casualties, they continued fighting over into the next day, until they had succeeded in containing the German's bridgehead across the Rhine. It had been a vicious fight, but the Rainbowmen had fought valiantly in their first major battle of this war.

When he wrote his next brief letter, Private Forehand, heavy mortar crewman, had seen and heard more than he would care to tell, and he couldn't tell it if he wanted to anyway. Neither would he want to say anything that would cause Hazel to worry about him, so he hurriedly jotted a few lines just to let her know he was okay, that was all she really wanted to know. He couldn't tell her that they had received word that a column of German tanks was headed their way, and of the tension and fear that had gripped him during the hours of waiting; as it turned out the column of tanks never showed up, thank God.

CHAPTER TEN

On the Maginot Line

#14, January 6, 1945
France

Dearest Sweethearts:

Just a few lines to let you all know I'm getting along fine, surely hope you all are ok. Honey, it's pretty cold here, there's some snow on the ground, it reminds me of when I was in California in '39. I'm staying in a pillbox in the "Maginot Line", and its really built for protection, so don't worry about me. I've nothing to worry about when I lay down at nite to sleep. Darling, I heard from "Buck", he spent Christmas in (name of place marked out by censor). Time passes awfully fast over here. I'll sure be glad when my time is up here too. Well, Dear, I'll close, so be sweet and write often. Tell babies Dada is ok and will be home some day.

Love, Dada

The "Maginot Line" or "Supertrench" as some called it, was a line of heavy fortifications built by the French after almost losing to the Germans in World War I. To make their border harder to penetrate, they built, beginning in 1930, an 87 mile long string of underground forts facing Germany. It took 7 years to complete the fortifications, and it was named after Andre Maginot who was the Defense Minister of France when the work began. It was an awesome line of layers of defense; at its forward edge were tank traps, behind which lay barbed wire and pill-boxes. Next came rows of gun emplacements walled in 10-foot thick concrete and armed with machine guns and anti-tank weapons ranging from 37mm to 135mm. At 3 to 5 mile intervals were located huge fortresses, buried as deep as 100 feet underground. Inside these forts, up to 1200 men could live for 3-month tours. These forts were all interconnected by tunnels with electric trains to allow rapid movement of troops from one place to another. There were comfortable underground sleeping quarters, bathrooms, kitchens, everything needed for the comfort of French soldiers. However, the Germans, in their blitzkrieg attack on France, at the beginning of the war on the western front, attacked around the end of the line, through Belgium and Holland, and flew over the Maginot Line, dropping thousands of paratroopers behind the line in France. The guns of the Maginot Line could not be turned around the other way to fire on the Germans, so they had easily defeated the French, and fought their way into France.

But now, the Allied Forces had fought their way north through France, sending German troops back across the line, and among other units defending the Maginot Line was the 242nd Infantry.

So when Forehand wrote that he was in a secure place, he was in a place "really built for protection". He had also been given the job of company barber, and was paid 25 cents per haircut by enlisted men and 50 cents by officers, which kept him in some change to rattle in his pocket. Too bad there was no store anywhere nearby, or he could have found something to satisfy his sweet tooth; he had candy on his mind when he wrote his next letter.

> #15, January 8, 1945
> France
>
> Dearest Ones:
> Just a few lines to let you all hear from me, I'm getting along just fine, hope you all are ok. I dreamed of you all last nite, and I sure do wanta see you all. We have mail call about twice a week, so I hear from you all about every four days. Darling, if you can find any good crispy peanut candy bars, send me a box of them. I'd also like some good home cooked candy. Be sure you pack them in a good strong pasteboard box. I've never gotten my fruit cake yet, but I'm gonna stay here for a while, so maybe it'll catch up

with me. There's a heavy snow on the ground, but it's not so cold. I've slept in everything from a hotel to a foxhole, feather beds, and on the frozen ground. I'd just about as soon sleep on the ground, it don't bother me any more. Well, Sweetheart, I'll close, all be sweet and write often.

Love, Dada

The Battle of the Bulge was still raging in the Ardennes. It was a fierce battle, this largest land battle of World War II in which the U.S. forces fought. The casualties were great; by the time this battle was over, American forces alone would have suffered 81,000 casualties, with over 19,000 killed.

In the bitter cold, freezing rain, then snowstorms with gale winds, as many soldiers were withdrawn from battle due to exposure as from injuries sustained in battle. Many local people opened their homes to the American soldiers and offered them warmth, food, and fuel, and helped comfort the ill and nurse the wounded. In the snow, the enemy attacked wearing white suits, even tanks were painted white, making it that much more difficult to see them. But the Allied forces fought on, not giving up hard-won ground, even though the price in lives was heavy.

Meanwhile, back on the Maginot Line, the 42nd Division continued to hold off the Germans, who had launched an attack on January 5 against three small towns to the north of Strasburg, aimed at forcing the Allies to withdraw. But after the bitter battle that lasted two days, when the Rainbow division had contained the Germans' bridgehead across the Rhine, they knew the Germans would look for another place to attack.

Forehand, with the 3rd Battalion, was positioned outside the town of Hatten; today he had watched as an Allied plane shot down a German 190. After a meal of cold rations, he jotted off a short note to Hazel to send out in the next mail dispatch.

#16, January 9, 1945
France

Dearest Wife and Babies:

I'll try and ans your sweet letter rec'd today. Sure was good to hear from you all and to know you are all well and ok. It was written Dec. 23, a few days before xmas. A few boys got boxes today, maybe I'll get mine soon. Darling, I'm still getting along good, hope you all are okay. Guess I'll be 24 when you get this. Wish you could cook my dinner. Please tell Mama I was thinking of her yesterday, her birthday. Just ate my good chow, chilled. I think of you all, wishing for the day when I can come back to you. Saw a P-47 and a German 190 tie up, the P-47 shot the 190 out of the sky, made us feel good. Well, Sweet, I'll close, ans soon.

Your loving Dada, BF

CHAPTER ELEVEN

The Rainbow in Hatten

On January 9 the Germans made the mistake of attacking the French town of Hatten, which was being defended by the 242nd Infantry. 1,050 well-armed enemy troops, all combat veterans and known as some of the best in Hitler's army, began attacking, in white uniforms and with white tanks, early in the morning. The men of the 242nd counter-attacked furiously, even in house-to-house combat as the enemy came into Hatten; and they held their ground even when tanks and personnel carriers surrounded a large Maginot pillbox they were defending. The 242nd had laid anti-tank mines across the streets of the town, and the tanks were too far into Hatten to retreat; the fire fight was intense, even cooks and headquarters personnel grabbed rifles and machine guns and got in on the fighting, which continued until midnight. Assaults began again at daybreak, and came throughout the day from every side of the town, but the 242nd continued to defend their positions. The battle for Hatten finally ended on January 11; the Rainbow had fought fiercely and stopped the Germans in Hatten, so fiercely that German officers who were later captured expressed amazement at how hard the Rainbow infantrymen had fought, and that it was the best infantry defense they had ever seen.

In the ferocious fight in Hatten, the battalions of the Rainbow Division suffered heavy casualties, especially the First Battalion, of which nearly two-thirds of its men were either killed or wounded or listed as missing in action. In an effort to replenish the devastated First Battalion , the men of the other two battalions were offered a raise in rank if they were willing to transfer to the First Battalion; in effect, volunteers would be raised to the rank of Second Lieutenant, a "battlefield commission," if they would make the change, which of course would mean a change in comrades, among other things. Forehand thought about the benefits of making a change, then decided to stay with his outfit, they had worked together good up to this point, and he just wanted to stay where he was.

Although Private Forehand had seen and heard many things he could not talk about in a letter home, he knew Hazel counted on hearing from him. Even though he was exhausted, just writing the few sentences, just putting it down on paper, seemed to confirm the reality that he was still alive and able to continue to communicate. If he ever had doubts that he would make it out of this war alive, he never expressed it in his letters; his wife must not sense fear in the words he wrote to her, he knew she had enough to cope with without thinking that he may not make it back home to her.

> #17, January 11, 44
> (Actually 45)

Dearest Ones:

Just a few lines to say hello. Wonder how you and our sweet babies are tonite? Sure hope you all are okay, as for me I'm getting along just fine. I dreamed of you all last nite, I'm afraid you are sick but hope not. Darling, don't worry about me. I stay far enough back that I'm pretty safe, what time I'm not in a pillbox, I'm under the ground. I feel sure I'll be with you all again before long. I'm glad C.D. got home. Maybe Roy will be next. Nites here are 14 hours long, I need 14 hours sleep, so I'll close and get started. Write often,

> Love, Dada

Forehand still had not heard whether his wife had given birth yet to their third child, and daily wondered whether he was father of another daughter or if this time it was a son. He had received a couple of letters from Hazel last night at mail call, but since the letters were written more than three weeks earlier, they didn't mention a new baby, so he continued to wonder.

Hazel's latest letter mentioned that C.D. had returned home from the war; it was C.D. who had driven them in the paperwood truck to the courthouse a few years earlier. "I'm glad he made it back home," thought Forehand, hoping they could say the same for him before too

long. He had seen a lot of good soldiers go down in recent fighting; it made him more determined than ever to do his best to stay alive and make it back home, the sooner the better.

#18, January 13, '44
(Again, really '45)
France

Dearest Wife and Babies:
I will ans your sweet and welcome letters I rec'd yesterday, of Dec. 15 and 22nd, this leaves me getting along just fine, surely hope you and my sweet babies are still well and getting along good. I'll sure be glad when I find out how you got along, and how the little baby is, I wonder if it's a boy or a girl. We get candy, chewing gum, and cigarettes every day, costs nothing, the boys are getting more cigarettes than they can smoke. Well Darling, you all be sweet and don't worry about me, I'll be ok, tell all the folks hello, I'm too lazy to do much writing. Give my love to my darling babies.
Love, Dada

With each meal or k-ration the GI's were given a small package of four cigarettes; Forehand wasn't a smoker himself, just hadn't ever got started on the habit and didn't intend to do so now; so he was glad to give his cigarettes to other GI's .

The next morning Forehand stood outside in the snow eating a k-ration breakfast. They didn't get a hot meal this morning, but this meal in a small flat box was at least filling: a small can of egg and ham mix, some little biscuits, a fruit bar, plus the usual pack of four cigarettes, matches and toilet tissue. He had heard that the news was everywhere about the Rainbow's victory at Hatten, and while he was sure proud of the infantry and proud to be part of it, he was also proud of the U.S. planes that supported the ground battles by bombing and strafing German positions.

Going back into the darkness of the Maginot pillbox, he lit a candle and sat down for a while to answer the letter he had received last night from Hazel and the girls, a letter she had written on Christmas day, telling him all about their Christmas, how the girls loved their presents, and how they had all missed him being there. Even though her letter had taken three weeks to get to him, reading it today made him almost feel as if he had been there.

#19, January 14, '45
France

Hello Sweethearts:
Here I come in ans to your sweet letter of Dec. 25 I received last night. Yes, honey, I'd sure liked to have been there when the ladies got their little tea cups I sent them. I can just about see Jan Von pouring coffee for her babys. How did Peggy like her things? I tried to get the things that I thought they would like, that they might have a good Christmas. I spent mine down on the Rhine. I'm writing this by candlelight in a pillbox on the Maginot Line. It's 11 a.m. but it's always as dark as nite in here. It's pretty safe, too, that makes me like it. Well, Darling, the infantry still gets lots of publicity, and we have the toughest job, but it makes a man feel mighty good to see the air force up there. I stood in snow eating my k-rations this a.m. and watched our P-47 bomb and strafe the Germans. I'm getting along fine, hope you all are okay.
                    Love, Dada

On January 16 the Germans launched a new attack on the town of Sessenheim, about seven miles south of Hatten, this time using a thousand young fanatical troops who were some of their best soldiers. Supported by six huge Tiger tanks, the fanatical German troops attacked, and the fighting continued for several days, with heavy artillery, mortar, and automatic fire ongoing. Rainbow troops, along with infantry of the 79th Division, fought their way out into the woods; when they left the woods the next day moving back toward the town, the huge German tanks opened fire on them. The Rainbow and 79th withdrew, and received orders to withdraw to the Moder River near Hagenau to set up new defenses there.

Private Forehand had written on the 16th of moving from a pillbox into a foxhole in the woods; he had even built a small fire in front of the foxhole, and was sitting there trying to stay warm when he wrote Hazel . . .

#20, January 16, 45

Dearest Wife and Babies:

I wonder how you all are getting along today? Fine I hope, as for myself I'm getting along just fine. I'm just sitting around a good fire in front of my dugout thinking of you all, you should see my house, it's a pretty good place to live, it's warm and it's shell-proof, only took me and my buddy about 3 hours to build it with shovel and clubaxe. I'm sleeping about 12 hours each nite, getting plenty to eat, too. I hear plenty of noise but I see very little. Honey, I had a letter from Bea of Jan. 4, and no boy yet, don't try to put it off till I come home, it'll probably be a year. It must be twins, hope so. I've just been issued a fur lined jacket and boy it's sure warm. Darling, send me a ready addressed V-mail "no stamp" each time you write. I'll close so be sweet and write to Dada often.

Worlds of love, Dada

Unknown to Private Forehand, his wife had finally given birth, on January 15, to a third daughter; but it would be some time before the news would reach him on the line. The 242nd Infantry, along with other regiments of Task Force Linden, was placed now under the direct control of the 79th Division and began their withdrawal to the Moder River near Haguenau. Forehand wrote home again . . .

21, January 19, 45

Dearest Wife and Babies:

Just a line to let you all know I'm okay, surely hope you all are getting along just fine. The last letter I had from you all was written Dec. 25, I just had a letter from Bea of Dec. 5th. Mail is a problem over here. I can write four more V-mails, maybe you'll start sending me one each time you write, huh? It's stopped snowing and started raining here, it's sure getting muddy and nasty, too, I'd rather have snow, but I'm doing lots of things I don't like, so I'll put up with the rain and mud. Honey, write Leroy and tell him the name of the last town I wrote you I was in, send him an envelope and paper, ready addressed to me, ask him to tell me how far apart we are. I'm not in the town but I'm not too far off. I'm getting pretty plenty of sleep, pull two hours guard every night, and stay in the sack the rest of the night, sometimes there is so much noise I can hardly sleep, but I'm getting used to that, too. Well, sweethearts, I'll close, so you all be sweet, I'll write often. Answer soon,

Your loving Dada

The next day, January 20, was freezing cold, below 20 degrees, rain had turned to ice on the roads, and now it was snowing heavily again. The infantrymen were exhausted from days and nights of constant moving and steady fighting. Even traveling slowly, trucks and tanks and pieces of artillery would slide off the road into ditches, ravines and streams, as they began under cover of darkness their withdrawal as planned. The Germans must not have been expecting the withdrawal, so missed an opportunity to attack the infantry as they moved along the ice-covered roads. Forehand couldn't help but laugh when he saw other Rainbowmen slip and fall on the ice, until he lost his footing and fell a few times himself; even to walk a few yards without falling was not easy. After the walk of several miles under such conditions, and not having slept in a day and a half, it was a tremendous relief to reach their destination. But before crawling into his sack to rest, Forehand wrote another letter to Hazel, he wanted to let her know he had finally received his long-awaited package just yesterday before they started the all-night hike.

Letter #22, January 21, 45

Dearest Wife and Babies:

I've just read a letter from you all dated Dec. 7. Yes, mail is a problem over here. Well, darling, I finally got my cake, kerchiefs, and nuts; boy, it was really good, too. I got it yesterday, gave a piece of the cake to each of my section, 15 men, they sure bragged on your cooking, but I kept plenty of it to fill me. I sat out in the snow, made coffee, and really enjoyed the good cake. We walked about (censored) miles on a frozen road last nite, I had lots of fun for a while seeing the men slip and hit the ground, but it soon ceased to be funny, after I busted myself a few times. Well, sweethearts, I've not slept any for 36 hours. I'll close and get in my sack. So be

sweet and may God bless you all for me. Good nite,
sweethearts, write often.

Love, Dada

CHAPTER TWELVE

Haguenau

For the next couple of days, the infantry divisions moved into position and began organizing and strengthening their defenses around the city of Haguenau. On the southeast edge of the city, the 242nd occupied bombed-out buildings, and on January 24, Forehand wrote another letter home as he sat by a heater in a cold basement. At least he had been able to have a nice hot bath the night before, and had slept well.

Letter #23, January 24, 45

Dearest ones,

Will ans your very sweet letter I rec'd yesterday of Jan. 7, sorry you were so sick, sure hope the baby is born and you are feeling better by now. Glad my ladies were ok. This leaves me feeling fine, hope you all are ok. I took myself a good hot "douche" (bath) last nite, put on new underwear, and got a good nite's sleep. It's 9 a.m. and I'm just sitting around in a basement of an old bombed out building by the heater. Darling, I can't tell you what army I'm in, but you know about where I'm at, so you should be able to guess it, I'm close to a town that sounds about the same as Mac Segrest's wife's name. You can ask me any questions you want to, I'll answer most of them. There's lots of snow on the ground here. I'm getting plenty of gum and candy now. Well honey, I'll close and wash my sox, so don't worry about me, I feel safe. Be sweet, tell my ladies Dada is coming home before very long. Write often,

Dada

It snowed again that day and snow was now a foot deep on the ground. The temperature was well below freezing and many of the men in the infantry divisions were in foxholes half-filled with water and a crust of ice. If the German forces were able to capture the town of Haguenau, they would gain access to the roads south; the Rainbow infantry would fight hard to keep that from happening.

At 1800 the Germans began shelling the smaller towns around Haguenau, but the Rainbowmen fought them off for 24 hours and forced the Germans to withdraw. Just before dawn on January 25, The 242nd was attacked by the 10th Panzer Division SS troops, one of Hitler's best outfits. Forehand's battalion, the Third, was the brunt of the attack which was around a factory that the Germans had captured across the Moder River. In the late afternoon, the 242nd, with tank support, launched an attack that forced the enemy to break and run as gunfire from the infantry and tanks cut them down. The Third Battalion had inflicted high casualties on the enemy, killing around 400.

The battle of the Moder River was the last German offensive action on the western front, and the Rainbow infantrymen had stopped it. It was actually the turning point in the German campaign in Alsace; if the Germans had been successful, the Allies would have had to withdraw along the entire Army front.

The battle for Haguenau was over and the Germans had not been able to take the city; it had been another bitter battle for the Rainbow Division. They had been fighting tough battles for a solid month, and had lost equipment and half of their riflemen. On the 27th of January, they began moving back from the front lines to a reserve position to reorganize and to wait for the rest of their division, which had landed in Marseilles on January 18 and was preparing to move north and join them. And the Rainbow infantrymen needed a few day's rest; they were dog tired.

CHAPTER THIRTEEN

Rest, Regroup, Replacements

The infantrymen were moved into small towns which were heavily damaged by fighting, most of the buildings having no roof or windowpanes. They found the best of the battered buildings, boarded up windows and dug out stoves from the ruins, and at least were able to sleep on the floor in a warm room, which was as good as a feather bed after a month in ice-filled foxholes. While living in the cellar of one of the buildings, Forehand wrote another letter home . . .

Letter # 24, January 26

Dearest Wife and Babies,
Just a few lines in ans to your sweet letters I received a couple days ago, dated Dec. 27, 29, 30, and Jan. 2, this leaves me getting along just fine, sure hope you all are ok. The snow is about a foot deep and is still falling; I'm sitting around a heater in the cellar, thinking of the place I'm gonna try and own when I get home. It's gonna be in South Fla., a small home I'll make myself, and about a 40 acre farm to rent in the share crop plan, plenty of hogs and cows, a good saddle horse. If nothing happens to what we now have, we should be able to get just that, too, uh, honey? Well, sweetheart, I don't see why I can't write where I'm at, we wear our (insignia), the Germans know we're here. Remember the town Buck was in? How far, and in what direction did we find the blankety-blank? Honey, I'm safe here, so don't worry about me. Write to Dada often.
Worlds of love, Dada

The Rainbow Division had suffered many casualties in battle; now replacements began arriving and a training program was under way eight hours a day, including night operations. They also had movies for relaxation, and the men themselves prepared shows for entertainment. Forehand's next letter home is written on his 24th birthday . . .

Letter # 25, January 28

Dearest Sweethearts:

I'll try and ans your sweet letter I rec'd yesterday of Jan. 2. I hope you are all still ok, as for me I'm feeling fine and getting along good. Well, Darling, today is my birthday. To start it off, I went out on the "mortar" at midnight for two hours guard, some Krauts got out in front of our rifle companys and started digging in, the rifle men asked for fire, so the rest of my section came out to help fire on the Krauts. While we were shelling them, I told the boys I was 24 years old today, so they sang happy birthday to me while we were still firing on the Krauts. But don't worry about me, the only shells that come my way are "big ones" and I always have time to get in a hole, out of danger, as we can hear them coming in plenty of time to get out of their way. The snow is knee deep now, and it's still snowing. I dreamed of my sweet babies night before last. I'd sure love to see all of you, maybe I'll be home before too long. The boys are still singing to me, we have lots of fun. Well honey, I'll close now, be good, write often.

Worlds of love, Dada

In his next letter, written two days later, Forehand indicates they have been moving into a safer area away from the line of combat, and mentions having had a good night's sleep away from all the noise.

#26, January 30, '45

Dearest Sweethearts:

Just a few lines in ans to your sweet letters of Jan 10 and 12, sure glad to hear from you all, sorry you were feeling so bad, I know you've had a bad time since I left you all this time, sure would like to be there with you all, hope you all are ok now. As for me, I'm feeling fine and am getting along just as good as I did in the states. I really had a good night's sleep last night, no noise of any kind. We are as far from the line as it is to Lois' from home. We have a good room with a heater in it, so you see, I'm taking it easy since my birthday, don't worry about me, I'll be okay. Honey, I sure had a sweet dream of you last nite, only wish it could have been true, maybe it will be some day. I'll close, so be sweet and write often.

Love, Dada

During this time of training, the Rainbow Infantry awaited the arrival of the rest of their division. It was at least far enough away from the lines here that they could relax and unwind, although they were still busy with training, incorporating the newly arrived replacements into the regiments. Forehand assured his wife of his safety when he wrote again the last day of January.

#27, January 31, '45

Dearest Wife and Babies:

Wonder how you all are getting along today? Fine, I hope, as for me, I'm all ok. Honey, I sure do want to see you and our sweet babies, but it'll probably be a year before I see you all, but the time passes by

fast over here. I can't tell a Sunday from Monday. We have not been paid in 3 months today, but I don't need any money, there's nothing to spend it for. I keep my pockets full of gum and candy all the time. Sweetheart, I was in "Haguenau" my birthday. We've also been to "Hatten," these towns are up the Rhine from Strasbourg, in the Alsace sector. It sure is a relief to be out of range and hearing of the German 88s, no kidding! I'm as safe here as I was in basic, so don't worry about me. I'll close, so be sweet, write often. Hello, Peggy and Janice.
Worlds of love, Dada

The Rainbowmen had turned the town's taverns into mess halls, and were enjoying hot meals again, and even the luxury of a bath in the shower units that had been set up nearby. They knew they wouldn't be enjoying these comforts for very long, this war was still going on and soon they would be moving back into action. They had also finally received their pay, at least for the months of November and December; and Private Forehand, as some of the other soldiers, decided to send the entire amount to his wife, he had no use of it here anyway.

#28, Feb. 2, '45

Dearest Wife and Babies:
This leaves me feeling fine, and just as safe as if I was in the states. We are a good way behind the lines now just taking a rest, also for a bit more of basic training. So don't worry about me, I've been in combat and found out I'm in a good safe outfit. We have the rifle troops, our machine guns, and anti-tank troops between us and the jerrys, so we are pretty well protected from our foe. We've been

in combat since I wrote #23, and believe it or not, I haven't been up close enough to see the first German. I got paid today for Nov. and Dec., 1920 francs, about $39.00. I sent it all on to you, to put in the bank with the ladies' account, money's no good over here. How is yours and mine account coming on? Well Sweet, I'll close, so be sweet, write often.
                    Worlds of love, Dada
Hello Peggy and Janice! Pray for Dada.

After waiting anxiously for the news, Forehand finally received word that he had a new daughter, and that his wife named the baby Frances, in honor of her daddy fighting in France at the time. He could only wonder what his new baby looked like, if only he could see a picture of her it would all seem more real to him. He wrote to Hazel . . .

                              Feb. 6, 1945
                         Somewhere in France
Dearest Wife and Babies:
Just a few lines to let you know I'm still ok, hope you four are getting along fine. I surely do wanta see you all, seems as though Janice is still my baby, guess it will be that way till I see my little baby. Maybe if you can get to town and have a big picture made of Frances and send it to me, it would bring on a different feeling, also have new ones made of Peg and Jan, and send me as soon as you can, the big picture I have of us is good as ever, but the frame is about shot. The snow has all gone now, and it sprinkles most of the time, its pretty muddy, too, but not so cold. Darling, I guess I got

all your letters, I get one or more each time we have mail call, and I write every other day, most all the time. I've plenty of water repellent clothing and rubber boots. I get three hot meals a day, and now I'm learning radio and I don't like it much, but we have to have communications to fire our mortars. Well, Sweetheart, I'll close, be sweet, write often.

Worlds of love, Dada

Forehand's lips were so badly chapped from the wind and cold that they were split and sore, and made him wish for some Chapstick to soothe them. Then a Sergeant received a care package from his mother which just happened to include a Chapstick which he didn't want; he threw it aside, and Forehand picked it up, thankfully opened it and applied it to his sore lips, and pocketed it. Soon his lips were healed and he kept the Chapstick with him through the rest of the war.

The 242nd carried on with training, with emphasis on tactics of small units and tank and infantry coordination, as their recent combat experiences had shown them how important these issues were.

On February 6, Task Force Linden had officially been dissolved; the rest of the Rainbow Division was finally on its way to join with the three Infantry regiments, and would arrive within a few days. Forehand writes home again, "still taking life easy"..

#31, Somewhere in France
Feb. 7, '45

Dearest Wife and Babies!
Just a few lines to let you all know I'm still getting along okay, sure hope you four are well and ok. I'm still taking life easy, not doing anything but lying around and listening to this bunch of boys tell of their fights back home, in the jooks (country slang in the 40s for bars, jook referring to juke box)

113

and so on. I've been in my sack once tonite, couldn't go to sleep for their big talking. Honey I sure do wanta see my new baby. I know she's bound to be pretty. So hurry up and send me some pictures of her, write me all the news about Peggy and Janice, and what they think and say about Frances. I sure hope your health improves. Do you feel like caring for the three ladies. I know you have a time, but I'll be with you to help you some day. It won't be too long, I hope, as time passes fast over here. I'll sure be glad when "I can get seasick again". Well Sweethearts, I'll close, so I'll say goodnite to you four, write often with long letters. Kiss all the ladies for me.

Your loving Dada, BF

Note: Letters #32-34 are missing; perhaps lost along the way, as was Letter #29.

CHAPTER FOURTEEN

Complete 42ⁿᵈ to the Front

By February 10 the rest of the men of the Rainbow Division had arrived in the area and joined in the program of training; now the entire 42nd Infantry Division was officially in France. Four days later, on the 14th of February, the 42nd received orders to move into the front lines, relieving the 45th Infantry Division in the Hardt Mountains northwest of Haguenau. The couple of weeks of training would pay big dividends in the months ahead, as the Rainbow would see a lot more action. And on the Valentine's Day, after a day of riding around observing a number of flattened French towns, Forehand found a comfortable place to sit and write again to Hazel and the girls.

#35, February 14

Dearest Wife and Babies:

I'll try and answer your sweet letter I've just rec'd of Jan. 30, mailed Feb. 2nd, sure glad you and the ladies were getting along good, this leaves me getting along just fine. We went on a training problem today, seen about 15 more of these French towns, or what's left of them. Most of these towns are lying flat, the bread the people eat is "hard black" bread, but hungry people will eat anything. I'm sure glad Peggy is smart and a big girl, so she can help you look after Jan Von and Gerome (baby Frances' middle name), she can write good too. I'll sure be glad when I can help her to write. I've not been up front since my birthday, we don't do nothing but eat and sleep, we have lots of fun, of singing and talking. I'd sure like to have my guitar, but no chance. Well, honey, I'll close, so be sweet and write often. Hello to Peggy and Janice and Frankie.

Worlds of Love, Dada

The next morning, February 16, the Rainbowmen who had already been in combat were awarded the Combat Infantryman's badge. Orders were given for the move back into the lines, equipment and personal belongings were readied, and that evening they began moving. As they moved forward, Forehand now was carrying in a canvas bag on his back a heavy field radio for mortar communications. Along the way he slipped and fell down a ten-foot ravine by the road, but was uninjured and climbed back up out of the ravine and continued the march. When in their assigned positions, the Division covered a front eight miles long. Major General Harry J. Collins was put in command of the Division on the 17th, and on that day the entire Rainbow Division began its first day of combat as a unit in World War II. General Collins wanted his men to be aggressive, so he sent them out on patrols and raids to gather information on the Germans' location and strength. Front line infantrymen dug their foxholes, and the rest of the infantrymen were billeted in houses or empty buildings. Forehand wrote another letter to Hazel before they began their move into the lines . . .

February 16

Dearest Wife and Ladies:
Will ans your two sweet and welcome letters I rec'd last night, of Jan. 27 and Feb. 6th, sure glad all was well, this leaves me ok. I hope you four are still ok. Our Colonel came out this morning and awarded us with the "Combat Infantryman's Badge", so if you wish, you can get one next time you are in Panama City or Mariana and wear it. Honey, I wrote you about a month ago to send me a V-mail "without stamps" each time you write, why didn't you start doing this? It'll probably be a month before my package with V-mail gets here, I can't buy it here, and I've borrowed all my writing material lately. Guess I'll have to stop writing so

regular, ok? I dream of you and babies most every nite, sure do wanta see you all. The "marked out" place was Strassbourg. Well, Honey, I'll close, ans soon.

Your loving hub and dada, BF

Hello Peggy, Janice, and Frances

When the Rainbow Division moved into the lines they were opposed by a German division that was well trained in fighting in the mountainous terrain they were now in. The enemy had laid thousands of Shu-mines that exploded when stepped on and caused serious injuries. The Rainbow laid their own mine fields and booby traps against enemy patrols, and for the next 11 days carried out extensive reconnaissance and combat patrols, during which they inflicted casualties on the enemy, but also suffered casualties, mostly from enemy mines. Each of the regiments had lost men, some killed, some wounded, others missing in action. The Rainbow was supported by artillery of another mortar battalion, the 83rd, and the artillery was so strong that a captured enemy admitted they were afraid to fire their guns, knowing it would bring a quick response from the "terrible artillery". The feared U.S. artillery included secret shells containing radar devices in the nose that could be pre-set to explode a certain distance above the ground.

Forehand and his section spent the night of the 17th bedded down in a hayloft, but the following day they moved into a vacated house. He was thinking back over the events of the last several years when he wrote letter . . .

#37, 18th

Somewhere in France

Dearest ones:

Well, here I come again, hope you all are feeling fine this Sunday morning, as for me, I'm all ok. Well honey, Just five years ago today, I took you for my first ride in that little ole Ford coupe of mine, seems as if it were only yesterday. Lots has happened since then, three sweet kids and a pretty good start in life. Darling, I dream of you and babies most every nite, guess it's because I always go to sleep thinking of you all. I slept in a hay loft last night, sure slept good and warm too, have now moved into a good room with heater in it. Honey, don't worry about me, I'm safe here. Well, sweetheart, I'll close, so be sweet and write to Dada often.

Worlds of love, Dada

Over the eleven days in which the Rainbow Division carried out continuous combat and reconnaissance patrols, eleven Rainbowmen lost their lives—32 were wounded, 11 missing, most caused by mines. The Germans suffered more than twice as many casualties.

Private Forehand's letter could not indicate the reality of what was going on at the time; all he could write about was the beauty of the countryside and his desire to see his family again, and soon. He sat down and once again put his thoughts on paper.

#38, Still in France
Feb. 20, '45

Dear Sweethearts,

Here I come in ans to your sweet letter Feb. 7, I received last night, glad all of my four little girls were ok, this leaves me getting along just fine, hope you four are still ok. Darling, I'm sure glad you are in good health, I was afraid your health would be bad after the baby was born. I sure do wanta see her and all of you, but I don't have any idea when I'll see you again, I'm just hoping that it'll be soon. This is pretty country here, lots of pretty timber, and small mountains, kindly reminds me of Chimney Rock, the men that are in this town are 50 or over. I watched an old man make a pair of wooden shoes today, they sure look odd, want a pair of them? Honey, I'm not too far from the town I was in on my birthday, but I'm plenty safe here. I'll close, so all of you be sweet, write often.

Worlds of love, your Dada

The next morning, while his regiment was still in reserve, Forehand did his washing, at least his socks, hankies and underwear. When the mail was handed out later in the day, he finally received baby Frances' birth announcement card.

#39, Somewhere in France

Hello Sweethearts:

Just a few lines to let you all hear from me, this leaves me getting along just fine, surely hope my four little girls are ok. Well, Darling, I'm just laying around doing nothing but eating and sleeping. I washed my socks, hankies and underwear today. I'm a pretty good housekeeper, but I'll sure be glad when you can do my housework, while I play with the ladies. I'm glad you got my tax refund, have you had my last year's tax figured and sent off yet? Well honey, I've just heard we've got mail coming, so I'll wait a few minutes and see, then finish this. Well, the only letter I got was the arrival card of Frances Gerome, it's pretty, but don't you spell her name wrong? Francis is a boy's name, her name is Frances. I sure do wanta see her. Well sweet, I'll close

so be good to the ladies and to yourself.
Your loving husband and Dada, BF

Though Forehand's battalion is in reserve, they are near enough to the front that he hears the artillery and planes. His next letter home is written on a Sunday morning . . .

Feb. 25, '45,
Northern Alsace, France

Dearest Hazel, Peggy, Janice, and Gerome:
Wonder what my four sweet girls are doing this Sunday morning? I guess you are still sleeping, as it's only 3 o'clock back where you are. This leaves me getting along just fine, surely hope you four are ok. Honey, I've not heard from you for the last three mail calls, as it's all been v-mail, so from now on, please write one v-mail one day (or three) and air mail next, both usually get here in about ten days. Today is a bright sunshiny day, everything quiet, except our air corps and our artillery. I'm in reserve, so I've nothing to worry about, Jerry don't seem to have much artillery here. I don't think he can hold out much longer. Honey, if Falmer should happen to get home any time I'm away, let him use the car (not just once but several times). Who knows, I may never use it anymore, I'm hoping to, but you can never tell. Well, Sweethearts, I'll close and go to Protestant service. So be sweet and write often,
Lovingly, Dada

The enemy's morale was being battered by the heavy shelling and continuous patrolling of the American soldiers, so much so that some Germans began to desert their units and surrender to the Americans. Taking advantage of this situation, the Rainbow Division began on February 28 a program of 15 minutes of heavy artillery and mortars raining on the enemy positions, followed by firing leaflets and broadcasting a call urging enemy soldiers to surrender.

The Rainbow continued training seven days a week, eight hours a day; everyone hoped this war would soon be over, but they had to be ready to keep fighting for as long as it took to win this war, and they had to be at their best. Replacements continued to arrive and joined in the training; war was serious business, and each soldier knew it. He realized the next soldier killed, injured, or captured might be himself or his best buddy, and he was determined to do all he could to keep that from happening.

Foxholes and dugouts were home to the men during this time of training, but they were served hot meals, which made it more bearable. Shower units were set up behind the front lines, where the men could go for a shower and change of uniform. Socks were washed daily by men on KP duty, as clean dry socks were an important issue in preventing frost bite and also trench foot, which was a serious problem, as it had also been in World War I, and was caused by wet socks in wet boots for days on end. It was still rainy and muddy, but beginning to warm up a little from the bitter cold they had experienced for the past few months.

Because the terrain over which the Division would be moving was very rugged, entirely wooded and steep tall mountains, it would be a difficult advance, especially moving equipment in an area with very few roads. Knowing this, before the end of February the 513 Mule Pack Company was assigned to the Rainbow to help move supplies needed, and infantrymen were trained to handle and load the mules.

The army knew that the soldier's morale was all-important, and part of keeping up morale was making every effort possible to get the soldier's mail from home to him. It was his keeping in touch with home and family that kept many a soldier going when he was under the pressure of combat, and fueled his desire to make it through this battle and the next one and till this war was over.

On "Friday night, March 2, 1945—Somewhere in France," Forehand was thinking of home and his family when he took out a regular size sheet of paper and sketched the house he wanted to build when he got back home after the war. He sketched in detail and with precision, and when he was satisfied with the way it looked, he wrote a letter to Hazel on the top part of the page.

Friday night, March 2, 1945
Somewhere in France

Dearest Sweethearts:

Wonder how my four girls are getting along tonite? Fine, I hope, as for me, I'm all okay, it's pretty cold here again, snowing a bit, but don't look for a heavy snow now. I'm doing nothing but lying around, and as you can see, doing a bit of post-war planning. Decided to send plans to you and let you see the house "we're gonna build", I hope. What do you think of the plan? It's a long time off, but maybe we'll get to it by and by. One thing sure, it's gonna be a long ways from Kinard. I'm gonna build it myself, with the help of Hazel, Peggy, Janice, and Gerome, ok? I can still see you, Peggy, and myself as we built the little shack you're living in now. Well, Sweets, I'm sleepy, so I'll stop, hoping to hear from you all soon. So take care of yourself, and our three little daughters.

Your loving hubby and Dada, BF

At the next day's mail call, Forehand received a copy of their hometown newspaper, the County Record, in which he read the announcement of his new baby daughter's birth and writes . . .

Sunday, March 4

Dearest Wife and Babies:

Will answer your letter I rec'd last nite of Feb. 15th, glad you and the babies are ok. I'm getting along just fine, but I'm sure lonesome, it's been a wet wintry cold day and I've spent the day sitting by the heater thinking of you four, hope you are all ok and not as lonesome as I am. Honey, I got the County Record announcing Gerome's birth, but as you already should know, I'm not in the section of France it showed me to be, I spent Christmas in Strassbourg and was in Hagenau on my birthday. When you see Mildred ask her if Grady is over here, if so, send me his address, I think I seen him a few days ago, guess Curtis will be home on furlough in a few weeks. Well, I may go home to stay when the Jerrys are finished, I hope so anyway. Guess you often wonder if your letters are censored, they are never opened. Well, Darling, I'll close so be sweet and write often. Kiss babies for me.

Love, Dada

The men were getting impatient to move on, tired of patrolling into enemy lines and then withdrawing. They waited for orders to move forward. Forehand had just received a letter from home this afternoon and was sitting in a warm room, "Somewhere in France," with his squad when he replied . . .

Tuesday nite, March 6, 1945

Dearest Sweethearts!

Will ans your sweet letter I rec'd this afternoon, of Feb. 12, surely glad you four were ok, this leaves me getting along, just hope you four are still ok. Took your V-mail 22 days to get here, from now on, write me air mail. I sure do wanta see my four little girls. I think of you every hour of the day and dream of you most every nite. I'm still just lying around doing nothing but eating and thinking of the day when I can get out of uniform and step in my ole civilian clothes again, I guess that's every serviceman's desire. Well, if I only can get back to you all, I still have my happiest moments ahead of me. I'm sitting with the rest of my squad in our room of a house built in 1893. Some of us are writing, some reading, and one of the boys is frying spuds. We are fed three good meals daily, but we have our mid-meals too. These fried spuds are really good too. Well Sweet, I'll close, so be sweet, write often. Hello Peggy, Janice, and Gerome.

Love, Dada

It has been three months since the 42nd Rainbow Infantry Division landed in Marseilles, and in those three months, their baths have been limited. Private Forehand's lack of frequent baths must have been a shock to hear about when his wife received his letter . . .

March 9, 1945

Dearest Wife and Babies:

Will ans your letter of Feb. 26 I rec'd last nite, surely glad to hear from you all and to know you were all well, this leaves me getting along just fine. I had a good bath today, my 5th one since I've been in France, we're supposed to get a shower once a week from now on, with a clean suit of underwear and sox, o.d.'s too, but I've got my underwear sewed to fit, so I do my own washing. I'm still wearing my 30" pants you had thought was too small, I still fill them up. Darling, I sure do get lonesome for you and our sweet babies. I've just got my box and it came in good condition, and boy the candy sure is good, haven't eaten any pecans yet, the candy is still good and crispy. Well, Sweethearts, I'll close, so be good, write often. Good night, mama, Peggy, Janice, and Gerome.

Dada

The following day the 242nd Infantry received orders to replace the 222nd on the line. They readied for the move, were in place on the line early on March 12, and began aggressive patrols which put fear into the enemy troops opposing them, so much so that a captured German soldier asked them if they were part of Roosevelt's SS. Forehand writes from the front lines . . .

March 12, 1945

Dearest Sweethearts,

I will ans your very sweet letter of Feb. 28 I rec'd this afternoon, was surely glad you four were ok, this leaves me getting along just fine, hope you all are still ok. Darling, I sure do wanta see you four girls, Peggy is a big girl now, I'll bet she don't cry any, she can really write good too. Tell her to write Dada every time she can, and to rock Gerome for

Dada and to be good to Janice. I'll be back with you all before long. Well, honey, it's now 1:30 a.m., I'm up front again. I'm about as far from the Jerrys as you are from Granny's, but I'm safe. I'm doing guard duty at the moment, but it's inside. We're in houses, some of which were built in 1830, we have a good setup here, I could be sleeping in a feather bed, but I prefer my sleeping bag down on the floor. Well, Darling, I'll close, be sweet and write often.

Your loving dada, BF

CHAPTER FIFTEEN

The Big Push

On March 13 the 42nd Division, as part of the Seventh Army, received orders to prepare to attack on the 15th. This would be the first attack by the entire Rainbow Division in World War II , an attack which would not be over until the end of the war. Their objective was to smash German defenses in the Hardt Mountains, taking the Germans by surprise and uncovering the Siegfried Line, then smash through the west wall. The endless patrols would pay off; the Division knew the enemy's strengths and weaknesses and the location of mine fields the enemy had laid, all of which would lessen American casualties.

Three divisions were preparing for the big push, and the sight of a long convoy of ambulances, a really long convoy, grimly pointed out the danger of the mission they were getting ready for. Fear and anxiety was a reality in these situations and Forehand was not alone in thinking, "What are we going into?" The same tenseness gripped all the young soldiers. But they were in this together, and they hoped to come out of this together, and their courage in spite of their fear motivated them to face the task ahead. They were as ready as they were going to get, it was left up to each man to ready his own mind, and each man had to face his fears. During the last watch of the night on March 15th when the big push would begin, Forehand heard a gunshot. He was on guard and was talking to some officers when the shot went off. A quick investigation revealed that one of the soldiers, overcome with fear of the battle just ahead, had shot himself in the foot, knowing he would be sent away from the front line for treatment of his wound.

At 0645 the 242nd began their assault, encountered extensive mine fields and were fired on, slowing their advance for a few hours; but they moved steadily forward and by night had captured the town of Baerenthal. The Rainbow battalions moved forward through the densely wooded mountains, encountering mines and booby traps, but capturing high ground and taking prisoners. Just advancing through the rough terrain required each man's total physical effort, but they could not stop, they had to keep moving. The enemy had felled huge trees across the trails and roads and laid mines on them, and the combat engineer units worked at a fast pace clearing the way for the advance of supplies and artillery and keeping the Division traffic rolling forward.

Along this rough haul pushing forward, one of Private Forehand's mortar team was injured and unable to continue without help. Forehand rushed ahead 100 yards, laid down his equipment which included the heavy mortar base, went back and helped his injured buddy move the 100 yards where he laid him down; rushed his equipment another 100 yards forward, and returned to bring the injured GI another 100 yards. He continued this going forward, back, forward, until at last they arrived to a point at which his wounded comrade could be given medical treatment. Forehand knew his buddy would have done the same for him.

By the third day of the assault, the Rainbow Division had reached their initial objectives, capturing towns and taking more prisoners. On the 18th of March, in the early morning hours, they began attacking again, hardly having rested for the three days, still working their way across the thick woods of the high mountains. Then the Third Battalions of both the 232nd and the 242nd Infantry, only minutes apart, crossed the border into Germany, making them the first unit of the VI corps to cross the German border, and also the first unit of the Corps to reach the Siegfried Line.

The Germans had for years been building these huge concrete and steel fortifications known as the Siegfried Line, or West Wall. The forts were well hidden and camouflaged, and made even more difficult to penetrate with huge piles of felled trees in front of the forts. It looked like an impossibility to cross this huge network of German defense; but the Rainbowmen, having come this far and over such rugged terrain, were up to the task. They knew the enemy they faced here was demoralized and afraid, the battalions defending the forts being mostly made up of old men and young boys who, once they were hit, would be easy to take as prisoners. They would have to get across the Saarbach River, the narrow river behind which lay the Siegfried Line. But they must also take two bridges which were covered by fire from the forts, and though they captured one of them, the second

bridge was fought with better forces who succeeded in blowing up the bridge, killing Rainbow infantrymen who had withdrawn underneath the bridge. The fight continued over the first bridge, with an intense German counterattack which drove the infantrymen holding it back across the River. The German troops fought bitterly, in spite of the fact that their communications had been destroyed and they had become more and more disorganized. The 42nd needed these two bridges because they led to the only good road going north through the Division zone, so plans were laid for a more intense attack on the fortifications.

On March 20 orders were given for the crossing of the Siegfried Line; the 222nd Infantry would open the attack in the early evening and the 242nd would follow just before dawn the next morning.

On March 21, Allied P-47 planes dive-bombed and strafed the forts in front of the Infantry, followed by a barrage of artillery. Infantrymen watched from their foxholes hoping that the bombing and shelling would cause the Germans to surrender. And as the Infantrymen began attacking the pillboxes, some Germans began surrendering, while others tried to escape in cars and trucks and horse-drawn artillery carts.

For hours into the night, Rainbow Infantry artillery rained on the Germans, destroying whole columns of German soldiers, equipment, horses, wagons, and vehicles. Infantrymen chased the Germans who were now on the run. After breaking through the Siegfried Line the Rainbowmen took more than 2000 prisoners within the first 24 hours, many of whom threw down their arms and surrendered, realizing they could not escape. Infantrymen rode captured horses as they led the lines of prisoners that stretched for miles.

During the following week, the Infantry regiments sought out enemy hiding in the woods and hills around the Siegfried, and Infantry engineers blew up the Siegfried fortifications. And in the town of Dahn, where over 800 prisoners were taken, the Division held an awards ceremony and planted the flags of the 48 states of the United States on German soil. The Jewish chaplain had Nazis clean up the city hall in which he then held a Passover celebration in the town hall, the first Jewish religious service in that part of Germany since the Nazis had taken over.

After nine days of heavy action around the Siegfried Line, Private Forehand finally had time to sit down with pen and paper to write. He was bone tired, but he needed to let Hazel know that he was okay, figuring she had read about the fighting in the newspapers, or heard it on the radio. Not yet able to say where he was, at the top of the page he wrote . . .

Somewhere in??

Wed. P.M. March 21, 1945

Dearest Wife and Babies:

Just a few lines to let you all know I'm getting along just fine, surely hope you four are well and ok. Honey, I hope you are not worrying about me, I'm not doing anything much but just lying around in these rolling hills and thinking of you all, surely do wanta see all of you. I'm hoping to see you all by this coming Christmas, but if I don't get to, I'll not be too badly disappointed. According to the papers, the Jerrys are on the run most everywhere, and I personally know they are on the run "Somewhere". I've seen things that will be hard to forget, but all my buddies are still with me, I'm lucky and plenty thankful I'm fighting with the weapons that I don't have to get any closer to the line than you are to Granny's. You can pretty well keep up with where I am if you listen to news and read papers. Well, Sweethearts, don't worry about me, I'm all safe and ok. Will close for this time, be sweet and write often.

Your loving hubby and Dada, BF

CHAPTER SIXTEEN

Inside Germany

Now that they were in Germany, the non-fraternization rules were put into effect for the soldiers, forbidding social contact with the Germans and only allowing conversation necessary for conducting business. This was a conquered country and neither side knew what to expect; the Americans knew the German locals were afraid of them and probably expected the soldiers to loot and rob as their own soldiers did when they conquered other countries. And the Americans knew there was still danger and hostile feelings towards them; but as they were respectful of the people in the small towns and villages just inside Germany, the local people returned the respect, seemingly grateful for the Americans freeing them from Nazi tyranny.

Not since the time of Napoleon, in 1806, had an invading army managed to cross the Rhine river. In an effort to make it at least more difficult, the Germans had blown the Rhine bridges; but in the town of Remagen, halfway between Cologne and Coblenz, the Third Army was surprised to find that the Ludendorff Bridge was still standing; and the famous crossing of the Remagen bridge became the first Allied bridgehead across the Rhine, on March 7, 1945, 139 years after Napoleon had crossed the Rhine.

Now, the Third Army had established bridgeheads across the Rhine River and the Seventh Army had done the same at Worms. The Rainbow Division was now assigned the mission of passing through the Worms bridgehead and pushing towards Wurzburg.

Private Forehand wrote his next letter, at least now he could plainly state that he was in Germany.

Somewhere in Germany
March 24, Sat. a.m., 1945

Dearest Sweethearts,
Just a few lines to let you all hear from me, I'm still getting along just fine. Sure hope you four are okay, it's been over a week since I heard from you all. Well, Darling, I'm well inside jerryland now,

and I must say Germany is a much better looking country than France, plenty of reasons, tho', France has had nothing but destruction for the last five years, while Germany has had only bombing, which didn't do any harm to small towns. Most of my buddies slept in town last nite, I slept up on the hill. The German civilians were passing out the drink to the boys. We've really traveled the last few days, and I didn't know there were so many German soldiers til they started surrendering. As you hear the P.W. bag, believe it, it is true. Well, Sweet, I'll close, don't worry about me, I'll be ok. Write often. I dreamed of you all last nite.

Love, Dada

While staying in a nice home in Dahn with several other soldiers, Forehand got a chance to write home, remembering that today was his middle daughter's second birthday. He wished he was home to celebrate Jan's birthday with his family.

March 27

Dearest Wife and Babies:
I'm awfully sleepy but guess I'd better drop you a line. Surely hope you four are ok, for me I'm getting along just fine. I'm staying in a good house, with pretty furniture, don't do nothing but lay around. When we move into a town, the civilians move in one end of the town and we stay in the other end, we don't associate with them at all. Well, honey, today is Janice's birthday. I've thought of you all, all day, sometimes it seems I'll go crazy if I can't see my babies, guess this war over here will be over

in a few weeks and I'm hoping to at least get home on a furlough, but there's lots of men over here that will most likely get home before we do, they deserve it though. Well, honey, I'm very sleepy so I'll close. Hope Granny is better. Write often, don't worry about me.

Worlds of love, Dada

The war in Europe appeared to be drawing to an end, but the war with Japan still raged, and these infantrymen knew that they could be sent on to fight in the Pacific theatre, although they hoped to be sent home on a furlough before shipping out to the Pacific. After the tough battle at the Siegfried Line, the days in Dahn were a welcome relief; the infantrymen realized they would shortly move on and they needed this time of rest to prepare for battles ahead. Not knowing how much writing he would get to do once they were on the move again, Private Forehand wrote to Hazel and the girls again . . .

March 29
Somewhere in Germany

Dearest Wife and Babies!
Wonder how my four sweet girls are getting along tonight? Fine, I hope, as for me I'm all ok. I'm still staying in a good house, taking life easy. As long as we were in France, we lived right in the same house with French civilians, gave the kids candy, gum, and any food we didn't want, talked and smiled with them, but now that we are in Germany, well, it's a horse of a different color. The German civilians move in one end of town, we live in the other. They're not allowed in the part of town we're staying in, neither are we allowed in their part of

town. They try to be friendly, but we have nothing to do with them. Darling, I sure do wanta see you four, I believe the war will end over here in a few weeks, but that still don't mean I'll get to go home, I'm just hoping I'll get home some time this year. Honey, have you got a package from me? Guess I'll close for now so be sweet and write often.

Worlds of love, Dada

CHAPTER SEVENTEEN

Into the Nazi Cradle

On the last Sunday of March, which was also Easter Sunday, two Regiments of the Rainbow Division loaded into trucks and began moving across the Rhine River and toward Wertheim, 125 miles away. Because of a truck shortage, Forehand's regiment, the 242nd, stayed behind in Dahn until the trucks could return for them. The long convoy crossed over the Rhine on a pontoon bridge, a convoy that took three days, amazing the German villagers who watched the seemingly endless string of vehicles pass through their towns, while the German army fled on foot or horseback or battered vehicles.

It made the villagers realize the war had to end soon, the German army was no match for the Americans.

On April 1 the 242nd Infantry Regiment began their move across the Rhine, with the First and Second Battalions riding on captured German vehicles and horses. Forehand's Battalion, the Third, waited for the trucks to return for them.

In the next several days, the Rainbow Division advanced into this cradle of Nazism, driving toward the city of Wurzburg, which was one of Germany's largest cities and a center of medical schools and art. A baroque city with many beautiful rococo buildings, Wurzburg was also the site of factories that made parts for German U-boats.

The Rainbowmen found the three bridges crossing the Main River to the city had been blown, and Engineers went to work building pontoon and Bailey bridges to get troops across. Some soldiers of the 222nd Infantry found a rowboat and made it across the river safely, and assault boats ferried more troops across later that day.

The Bailey Bridge was ready on April 4 for at least the movement of foot troops across the river, and the Rainbow regiments moved during the night into the city and at the break of dawn began their attack to take the city. Resistance was bitter; civilians, firemen and policemen all joined with the military in fighting, and snipers were hidden everywhere. Tunnels built under the streets allowed defenders to sneak around to the rear of the Rainbowmen and attack them. But the Rainbow fought their way further into the city, clearing buildings and capturing more than 2,500 prisoners.

When the first two battalions of the Rainbow had made it through Wurzburg, the 242nd entered the city and systematically searched every tunnel, cellar, and building for enemy who had not already been found and killed or captured. They walked around dead German soldiers as they advanced through the piles of debris that filled the city's streets. The once-beautiful city of Wurzburg was now a pile of rubble.

With the battle for Wurzburg over, the Rainbow Division now headed north up the Main River to Schweinfurt, a large city which was the center of the Nazi ball-bearing industry as well as other important industries that the Nazis depended on for war materials. They knew that Schweinfurt, because of the ball-bearing industry, was heavily defended by rings of 88mm guns that could be used against ground troops.

On a Saturday, Private Forehand sat on the hood of a jeep while waiting to move with his regiment, pulled out paper and pen and wrote a letter to his wife and daughters. He had not written them for several days and it could be several days more before he would get another chance to write.

He had received letters from them, and they would be eager to hear from him.

April 7, 1945

Dearest Sweethearts,

Will ans your sweet letters I've received for the past few days. Surely glad you four were well and getting along good, also glad Granny was better, hope she's back home by now anyway. This leaves me getting along just fine. I'm sitting on the hood of my squad jeep, enjoying the good sunshine in a German town, or what's left of it; each big town I've seen is lying flat from bombing, most of the small ones are blown down by artillery. Then there are some towns that display their white flags, and are left undamaged. Chickens are laying pretty good over here, I'm eating plenty of boiled eggs, too. I'll sure be glad when the pictures of

my baby get here, hope you had some made of you and
Peg and Jan, too. Well, Sweetheart, take care of you four
little girls, be sweet, don't worry about me, write often.
All my love, Dada

After capturing Wurzburg, the Rainbow headed for Schweinfurt, fighting against stubborn resistance but clearing towns along the way as they moved forward against fire. They decided to encircle the city of Schweinfurt, and cut off all exits to keep the enemy from escaping and getting ahead of them to build a larger resistance. To clear the way for ground troops, Allied air power was called in to wipe out the German artillery that ringed the town. Bombs were dropped from 192 planes, and when the 88mm guns opened fire on the planes, the Rainbow artillery counterattacked and destroyed many of the big guns.

On April 10, 242nd Infantry patrols found a way to get into the city through an area where the 88mm guns were not operational. At three a.m. on the 11th, the 242nd began moving into the city, with the 232nd and 222nd moving in from the north and the south , and the 12th Armored Division, which had been attached to the 42nd, covering the east side of the city.

Private Forehand and his mortar crewman with the Third Battalion entered the city; when fired on by burp gunners and 88mm's, they fired their mortars and forced the enemy's withdrawal. Now their objective was to race ahead and capture the bridge at the river; however, when they were only a couple of blocks from the bridge, it went up in smoke. Although the enemy had destroyed the bridge, he had also destroyed his only way of escape from the city.

As the three Rainbow regiments went into the city and knocked out opposition, they found the city almost completely destroyed by the bombing and artillery shells. But they discovered that the ball-bearing factories were still operating with slave laborers, who hugged and kissed the soldiers that captured the factories. The Infantrymen rounded up 3000 prisoners in the city and surrounding area. Since leaving Wurzburg, the Rainbow had captured 6,680 German soldiers, and cleared 100 square miles of Nazi territory.

By the tone of his next letter, Private Forehand's wife would never have guessed the action he had been involved in. He writes . . .

April 11, 1945

Dearest Wife and Babies:

Will try and ans your sweet letters of Mar. 26 and 28 I rec'd day before yesterday, surely hope you four were well and ok, sorry Granny was still sick, hope she's better by now. This leaves me getting along just fine and having fun every day. Surely do wanta see you four, almost six months since I seen you, hope it won't be that much longer before I see you all again. I have plenty of fresh eggs to eat, mostly boiled, but once in a while I get in somebody's kitchen and fry them. I also have fresh sweet milk, too, anytime I see a milk cow, I fill my canteen full. I'm not faring bad at all. I have myself a good "luminous dial" wristwatch, a 7 shot nickel plated 22 revolver pistol, and a dandy shot gun, wish you had the pistol, but I can't send it through the mail. No, honey, I never hear from Falmer except through Papa and Mama. Well, Sweethearts, I'll close, so be sweet and write to Dada often.

Your loving hubby and Dada, BF

For the next couple of days, the 242nd and 222nd Infantry regiments continued mopping up operations in Schweinfurt while waiting for orders.

With a Brownie camera he had liberated, Forehand and his buddies even took a few photos around Schweinfurt. Although the freed slave laborers were celebrating their freedom, the people of Schweinfurt were angry at the destruction of their city, but by the next day or two they began filling the streets and forming long lines for food. The mayor of Schweinfurt committed suicide by jumping from his office window.

On April 13, while still in Schweinfurt, the Division received the shocking news that President Franklin D. Roosevelt had died suddenly of a cerebral hemorrhage while taking a couple of days rest at his retreat in Warm Springs, Georgia. The Rainbow Division held memorial services for the President; one such service was held by the 242nd Infantry in the midst of the rubble of Schweinfurt. The battle-weary infantrymen met for the service in a bombed-out theater, with the colorful flags of the 48 states displayed in honor of the President. Private Forehand and other soldiers stood guard against possible sniper attacks. From an upper story window overlooking the solemn memorial service going on below him, Forehand watched as the infantrymen stood at attention while the Division chaplain prayed. It seemed almost surreal, having a funeral memorial service in the middle of a grey pile of debris in the center of this defeated city.

The President's sudden death was an unexpected blow, happening just when we seemed so close to victory in Europe. In the memorial service, General Collins spoke, saying that the Army and the nation had lost a great leader and friend, and were sad that he would not be with them to see the final victory which seemed to be so near at hand.

The Germans hoped the news of President Roosevelt's death would discourage the Allied soldiers and slow them down, but the Allies felt the nearness of victory and continued their rapid advance through Germany. Taking this war on to a victorious conclusion would honor the memory of the President who had led the United States as Commander-in-Chief for so many years.

CHAPTER EIGHTEEN

To Furth and Nurnberg

On April 13, the same day as the memorial services, the Rainbow Division received orders to take the cities of Furth and Nurnberg. The city of Furth adjoined Nurnberg, which was the Nazi stronghold. The city of Munich was the birthplace of Naziism, but it had grown in Nurnberg.

Because they expected a strong fight for Nurnberg, the Rainbow would be joined by several other Divisions, including the Third Infantry, the 45th Infantry, the 4th Infantry and the 12th Armored Division. They planned to strike quickly, so loaded onto trucks and jeeps and trailers and raced toward the cities. When they ran into stiff resistance in a smaller town along the way, General Collins decided to minimize Allied casualties by surrounding the enemy rather than a direct assault. When the enemy realized they were surrounded, some of them surrendered and others withdrew, and the Rainbow pushed on toward Furth and Nurnberg.

In Furth, there were more than 7000 enemy troops from various army units that had joined together to defend the city against the advancing Allied forces, as well as men of the Volkstrum, or folk army, who had trained to defend their city. They had set up roadblocks all through the city, derailed streetcars to block streets, and built barriers of logs and steel, as well as blown all the bridges. And they had been ordered to defend the city only until the night of the 19th and then to retreat to Nurnberg to enlarge the Nazi forces there for the expected fight with the Allies. But the Rainbow Division had advanced rapidly and began their attack in the early morning hours of the 18th. Under cover of artillery fire the Infantry crossed the Regnitz River into Furth, others crossed the twisted girders of a blown bridge, and Rainbowmen began clearing buildings and holding blocks of the city well into the night. Forehand's battalion entered Furth at three o'clock in the morning of the 19th. The city's burgomeister, or mayor, surrendered the city in the early morning hours, and the Rainbowmen began rounding up more prisoners, with 5,000 enemy surrendering by the time it was all over. The people of Furth began clearing the road blocks, and when given orders to turn in all weapons, they not only turned in guns, but also gas masks, helmets, uniforms, Nazi party armbands, anything that they thought might identify them with the German army. American soldiers thought it strange that the people seemed completely indifferent to the columns of their own men being marched away to prison camps; maybe the people figured the prisoners were luckier than many who had lost their lives in the battle.

Now that Furth was captured, which had been their objective, the Rainbow Division was ordered south to seize and hold crossings of the Danube River and await further orders, along with the 12th Armored Division and the 106th Cavalry. The Rainbow advanced southward into the area of the talked-about German "Redoubt", in the Alps, where Hitler planned to reorganize his army and continue the war. Along the way, the Rainbow captured towns, and the local people seemed relieved for their presence, rather than the SS troops who forced them to fight and would shoot them in the back if they refused.

In the race across Germany, there was not much time for writing letters. The last letter Private Forehand wrote to his wife was . . .

April 15

Dearest Wife and Babies:

Just a few lines to let you all hear from me. This leaves me getting along just fine, sure hope you four are ok. It's kinda rainy tonite, but I'm inside a pretty good house, and I don't have any guard tonite, so I should get a good nite's sleep. I've just finished milking the cow, so we could have milky coffee for breakfast. I could have sent you a lettergram tonite, but you'd probably think something was wrong with me, you should be getting a couple letters a week from me anyway. Today's my baby's third month birthday and not even a picture of it, sure wanta see you all. Will close, write often.

Worlds of love, Dada BF

Many of the Rainbow Infantry had walked every mile of this advance since crossing the Rhine River. On April 21 some walked and others were motorized, and they moved nearly 16 miles that day. They were tired from fighting day and night, but kept pushing themselves to get farther, knowing each day now was bringing them closer to the end of this war. They advanced rapidly over the next couple of days, making gains and capturing bridges. On the 23rd they were given orders to cross two rivers, the Danube and the Lech, near the small town of Donauworth, where they expected strong fighting because it was a defense outpost in the area of Redoubt. The terrain was rough, and existing roads were in bad condition and mined, so engineers had to move in first to clear roads of mines, fill in craters, and repair bridges. Fuel, supplies, ammunition, and food were relayed forward to keep up with the rapid movement of troops; and the service units were so efficient that the Division was never delayed once for lack of supplies. The men of the signal company worked day and night as well, to keep laying wire for radio communications as the command post now was constantly moving.

On April 25 the Rainbow Infantry began their assault on Donauworth. The Germans had not expected them to arrive so quickly, and though caught by surprise, they fought to the death in house to house combat, and when the fighting was over and the Allies had captured the city, they only took 17 prisoners.

The Rainbow Division was the first unit in the XV corps to reach the Danube River, in spite of the heaviest opposition and the poorest roads. They were to cross the Danube and head for Munich, the birthplace of the Nazi party.

It was shortly after midnight on the 26th that the 242nd Infantry began crossing the river on assault boats. As soon as their boats reached the opposite shore, the infantrymen jumped out and ran as shells burst around them, diving into craters, then jumping out again and running to another crater, until they were out of reach of enemy fire.

Once across, they headed for the Lech River, where they found all the bridges had been destroyed. The Lech River was a very swift-flowing river, which made it impossible to cross in assault boats. Infantry patrols looking for another way discovered a large steel bridge that had not been completely destroyed, only dropped into the water; so they began repairing the bridge to make it passable. Under enemy fire, engineers worked on the bridge, and even though several were wounded, they finished repairs late that night, and the Rainbow battalions began crossing. As the jeeps began crossing the bridge, a German plane began strafing them. Forehand felt the sensation of being riddled with bullets, and when they heard their order to leave the jeeps and get off the bridge, he jumped out with the others, then ran back to cut off the jeep's lights. He then ran toward a head high wall he saw nearby, scaled the wall and landed with a thud on the other side, then realized he was in a cemetery. His heart pounded, but he was relieved to discover he had not actually been hit, and shortly they loaded back onto the jeeps and completed their crossing of the bridge, all of them a little shaken at the close call.

The Third Battalion of the 242nd Infantry then went on to capture the town of Rain. The rest of the Division crossed the Lech on a Treadway Bridge that the engineers constructed beside the one they had raised out of the river. Now the entire Rainbow Division had made two major river crossings in a 24 hour period. Having made it through their last serious obstacle, they were now on their way to their objective of capturing Munich. They marched in heavy rains, but were eager to reach Munich and didn't want to slow down.

The autobahn leading into the city was the Rainbow's right boundary, with the Third Division on the other side. The 45th Division was on the Rainbow's left, its boundary leading through Dachau. The three Divisions were actually in a race to reach Munich. They had heard that there would probably be little resistance in Munich, that their most serious obstacles would be poor roads and blown bridges. The 42nd was instructed to let the 20th Armored Division pass through them to lead the attack south; but the blown bridges and roads filled with craters slowed the armored down and so units of the Rainbow continued advancing. In the early morning of April 29, as regimental combat

teams followed the armor southward toward Munich, the 42nd, the 45th, and the 20th Armored Divisions converged on Dachau. Although these soldiers had seen comrades fall in battle and other horrors of war, they could never have imagined what they would find in Dachau, and its sights, sounds and smells they would never be able to forget.

CHAPTER NINETEEN

The Liberation of Dachau

The concentration camp at Dachau was only ten miles north of Munich. Established in 1933 as a prison of wooden barracks and fenced in with barbed wire, it grew larger and larger as the years went by, and high dark gray walls enclosed it. The number of inmates increased dramatically as those who opposed Adolf Hitler or were even thought to oppose him, were incarcerated there, along with anyone of Jewish descent. Prisoners were not only Germans, but also French, Russian, Polish, Czech, Dutch, Norwegian, Danish, and many other nationalities; they were from every type of profession, every part of society, they were political prisoners. Dachau was more than a work camp; it was a death camp, the oldest and biggest death camp in Germany, and the most dreaded and notorious..

Some of the prisoners had been in Dachau for the entire twelve years till 1945; but many thousands had died there of starvation, disease and torture, many died in the gas chambers and had been cremated in the ovens of the crematorium.

Knowing the American liberators were on their way, most of the camp administrators and SS guards, more than 1400 of them, had fled the camp on the night before. But before fleeing the camp, the guards had gone through the prison killing important prisoners or those they especially disliked for any reason, and when that seemed too slow a method, they simply turned their machine guns on inmates and mowed them down in numbers, leaving more than 2000 dead in their last murderous spree. And even in their last few days, knowing their time was short, they had continued operating the gas chambers , but having run out of coal for the furnace, just dumped piles of bodies into open graves and even into the moat around the prison. Inmates were beaten, starved and brutalized by the guards who had lost all semblance of human decency.

Now on their drive to Munich, the 42nd Division and the 45th Division approached Dachau from different directions, and entered the camp. An advanced party of the 42nd's 222nd Regiment, consisting of several officers and led by Brigadier General Henning Linden riding in jeeps, entered the southwest entrance of the camp complex, where a representative of the Geneva Red Cross turned the camp over to General Linden, and SS Second Lieutenant Heinrich Wicker, a young German officer who had been brought to the camp only two days earlier, formally surrendered the camp to General Linden. Soldiers of the 45th Division attacked the camp from the east, where they had to overcome resistance from the SS Waffen troops that were trained and quartered there.

The Second Battalion of the 42nd moved in and began wiping out SS guards who refused to surrender and were firing on the Americans coming in.

What these American soldiers found in the huge complex of Dachau was so horrifying and disgusting that many of the soldiers were sickened, some vomited, many cried at the sights they found as they entered. The stench of dead bodies was overwhelming, and the sight of so many dead and so many emaciated human beings was beyond what they could have imagined.

When the first Americans entered the prison, the 32,000 inmates went wild with joy at seeing their liberators. They also joined in attacking any SS guards they found, some of whom had changed into prisoner uniforms to disguise themselves, but their clean undamaged feet gave them away, and they were attacked by the inmates who had been beaten and starved by these guards, and had seen their family members and friends murdered by them. Finally, to get control of the situation, Rainbow men fired shots into the air over the crowd, calming them down somewhat, then the Second Battalion began moving through the camp of horrors. Everything they saw only made them sicker and more disgusted and angry at the atrocities that had been committed in this camp. Some of the young soldiers were heard saying, *"Now I see why we have been fighting this war"*.

In boxcars on the railroad tracks running through the camp, soldiers opened the doors and found the boxcars filled with bodies of prisoners who had been brought in on the train and left to starve; the few who had tried to escape had been shot. Amazingly enough, one lone survivor was found in one of the boxcars, and he was picked up

by one of the soldiers and rushed to medical care. The other 2300 or so were unloaded and buried.

While the Second Battalion went through the camp, the other Rainbow men who waited outside the fence were also overcome with the realization of what had actually been going on for years in this camp. Forehand quietly watched as the skeleton-like victims were moved into areas for medical attention, and as food was rushed into the camp for the inmates. He knew he would probably never again see such a horrifying sight, and it was almost more than he could bear. He heard the joyful shout of prisoners—those who were able to shout—and as he was to comment years later, *"watched the happy ones come out, the ones that could come out, like skeletons walking"*.

The Rainbow Division was charged with the welfare of the 32,000 freed inmates. The Rainbow's commanding officer, Major General Harry J. Collins, who was so moved by what they had found at Dachau, went beyond the call of duty in making provision for the inmates, arranging to bring in not only abundant food and medical care, but even religious articles and kosher foods for the Jewish inmates, even money and clothing and other necessities. Because of the sympathy and compassion of the officers and men, most of the survivors were brought back to sufficient health so they could be released to return home.

With relief work now well under way at Dachau, the 42nd continued their drive to Munich. Having cleared Dachau of enemy resistance, the Second Battalion advanced toward Munich and by that night had entered the outlying area of Munich, thus becoming the first American unit to enter Bavaria's capital and the birthplace of Nazism. It was in Munich at the Berger Brau Keller, a beer hall, that Adolf Hitler had first made a grab for power in 1923. Now, 22 years later, this birthplace of fanatical Nazism would fall into the hands of Allies, only one week before the end of the war in Europe.Loc teatrum noste, nossu ium imilius, nostraet vis cont.

Locciam adducturnum. Natus talariu squempe ristio etientem, nunum ocupior unt. Icaveri tanunum ste egil utem patiquem siliisum

CHAPTER TWENTY

The Capture of Munich

The 242nd Infantry raced down the autobahn toward Munich, advancing 30 miles during the day. As they neared the Amper River, they caught up with the 20th Armored Division which was preparing to cross. Because the infantry and jeeps could cross the river more quickly, General Collins asked for the armored unit to allow them to pass through first and permission was granted. So on the morning of April 20 the 222nd and 242nd Infantry passed through the 20th AD and entered Munich. On the east side of the city the 45th ID was fighting some resistance, but the Rainbow met no resistance , and the 3rd Division also entered the city without resistance. Each of these Allied divisions entered almost simultaneously into Munich, but the Rainbow Division captured the center of the city, including the Rathaus beer cellar where Hitler organized the Nazi party years before, and the Koenig Platz where the Nazi party held their huge rallies each year.

Munich was a manufacturing center, and more than one fourth of the population were slave laborers. As the first Rainbow men entered the city, they went wild with excitement and, when they realized the German army was not going to put up a fight with the Allies, they began breaking into and looting the wine cellars and food warehouses, a sort of payback to the Nazis who had used them as free labor for years. Other Germans joined in the looting, while white flags of surrender began fluttering from windows throughout the city. Streets were filled with rubble and debris from bombing, and German soldiers began looking for places to surrender. The 42nd ID drove the looters away and placed guards on the warehouses, trying to bring some law and order to the lawless city. They began rounding up enemy soldiers and prisoners, and military traffic began filling the streets as rubble was cleared away. Long lines of thousands of prisoners were marched to a PW enclosure. Allied prisoners of war who had been forced to stay in boxcars during the bombing of Munich were released . Military officers moved into the Rathaus which was hardly damaged, and the burgomeister of Munich surrendered the city to them.

With the fall of Munich, the German army there and civilians considered the war to be over. As the thousands of dejected Germans, mostly men, were marched through the Munich streets toward the PW holding area, their hopes of a Redoubt, a retreat to the Alps to reorganize their army, were crushed, and they seemed to be sick of war. As they were leaving the city, the 242nd Infantry captured another 1500 German soldiers in a large airport south of Munich, as well as 500 German WACs and military buildings and equipment.

With the Brownie camera he had captured along the way, Forehand and his comrades took a number of photos of Munich and of themselves , now in a lighter mood at the relative ease of capturing the city. They looked for places of interest to take their photos, before loading into their jeeps and heading on to the border of Austria. As Popio, the driver of Forehand's jeep, followed the long convoy going toward Austria, Forehand continued taking pictures which he planned to take home with him soon.

He had also acquired a guitar in Munich that he would also take home with him. He loved the feel of a musical instrument in his hands again, after several months of holding weapons and mortar charges it was a nice change, a welcome change.

CHAPTER TWENTY-ONE

The War is Over

As they began the drive away from Munich, Forehand and the other infantrymen saw that surrendering Germans were lining the roads; entire companies of Germans surrendered, and some German officers signed orders for their soldiers to return home or told them to turn themselves in to the Allied army. Even generals and other officers drove themselves to surrender points as the German army broke up. The Rainbow men continued the huge job of rounding up prisoners and escorting them to the rear where they would be picked up and taken with the other thousands of PW to the enclosure.

On May 3 the Rainbow ID crossed the Inn River, and on May 4 they reached the Austrian border and patrols crossed over. They then received orders to move into assembly areas along the border, where they remained for the next few days, just north of the city of Salzburg. The Rainbow infantrymen were exhausted from the last three weeks of continuous marching and fighting and working; they were happy with the idea of just getting some good sleep, good food, and a good bath.

On May 7, the German army formally surrendered to the Allies, when at 2:41 a.m. German representatives surrendered in a schoolhouse in Rheims, France. The war in Europe was officially over, after 5 years, 8 months, and 6 days of war.

From the town of Tachinzerlee, Germany, on the border with Austria, Forehand writes . . .

May 7, 3 p.m.

Dearest Wife and babies:

Today I'm kinda lonely. The war is over, and now I'm wondering just when I'll get back to you four, but your guess as to when I'm coming home is just as good as mine. I rec'd your letter yesterday of April 22, sorry to hear of Ruel Smith's being killed in action, he went to Blanding and came to Ft. McPherson with me. I've had some pretty close calls, have seen several that have fallen, but I'm thankful to God that I'm still living in the best of health and am hoping to be home by Christmas anyway. Sorry my little baby has been sick, hope and pray she's ok by now. This leaves me getting along just fine. Hope you four are well and getting along good. I seen a movie this morning, we have a good radio in my room, it plays about 18 hours a day, the news from the Pacific sounds good, surely hope the japs will give up soon, I kinda believe they will. Well Honey, I'll close, tell the babies hello.

Write often, your loving Daddy, BF

Although the end of the war in Europe was not announced until May 8, the Allied soldiers knew it was over on the 7th, having heard of the surrender at Rheims.

On May 8, the New York Times headlines read: THE WAR IN EUROPE IS ENDED! SURRENDER IS UNCONDITIONAL; V-E WILL BE PROCLAIMED TODAY. OUR TROOPS IN OKINAWA GAIN.

In Paris, searchlight beams formed a V for victory in the skies over Paris. But V-E Day did not mean that World War II had ended, and although the level of excitement in the United States was high, Pres. Truman asked the American people to refrain from celebrating, and to dedicate themselves to the solemn task that lay ahead, referring to the war in the Pacific theater that still was raging. And in Germany, the Allied troops, while elated over the victory in Europe, also realized that they might next be sent on to fight in the Pacific.

On May 11th, the Rainbow Reveille newspaper explained the general attitude of the 42nd ID: "War in Europe found Rainbow men in the shadows of the Bavarian Alps, where they offered thanks to God for the end of hostilities and paid reverent tribute to their dead. There was no celebrating of the Times Square variety among GIs, but merely a feeling of thankfulness that one phase of the World War was finished. At Palling, in a service that was attended by liberated slave laborers and PWs of all nations as well as soldiers of the 42nd, Major General Harry J. Collins, Division Commander, thanked God that the Rainbow had accomplished its trying task with a minimum of casualties and told his soldiers how thankful he was for the job they had done so well." The Rainbow Division had seized over 6,000 square miles of Nazi held territory during their march across Europe. By the end of the war, they had established an enviable record, being the first in their corps to enter Germany, first to penetrate the Siegfried Line, and first into Munich. They had captured 51,000 prisoners, and marched more than 450 miles from the Hardt Mountains of France, over extremely rugged terrain, to the border of Austria, and had captured key German cities along the way, liberated Dachau, and spent 114 days in combat. Once again, the Rainbow Division, represented by every state in the union, had proven themselves to be first-class fighting men, and could feel proud to have upheld the reputation established by the World War I Rainbow men.

On Sunday night, Forehand writes Hazel from Krimml, Austria . . .

May 13

Dearest Wife and Babies:

Will try and ans your sweet letter I rec'd last nite of April 25. Sure glad you four were ok, as for me, I'm okay, except I'm kindly tired from riding most all day. I'm over one hundred miles from where I left this morning. Guess I must be about in the heart of the Bavarian Alps, we're in a good house, listening to Jack Benny's program at present. About a half mile south of me, and about 700 feet above me, there's a waterfall coming down off the mountain, it's sure pretty, it's plenty loud, too, has a much louder murmur than Willis Pitts' mill does. The mountains reach way up in the sky, they are all around us, they are wooded and most of them are covered in snow. Well, Sweethearts, I don't know as yet when

I'll be on my way to the good ole USA, I just hope it'll be soon. Will close and play the boys a tune on my guitar.
Good night, sweet ones, Dada

Though his letter was dated the 13th, it may have been written on the 14th, as that was the day the Rainbow made the move into Austria. Or his unit may have started earlier than some of the other units in the move.

Until May 14, the Rainbow Division stayed on the Austrian border near Palling, during which time they rested, and maintained equipment, but also had to help control the flow of refugees heading back home now that the war was over.

On May 14 the Rainbow moved south into the beautiful Tyrol area of Austria. There they began training for redeployment, but also helped round up thousands of German soldiers who had come to that area to make a final stand. Once they were relieved by the 20th Armored Division, the Rainbow began serving as occupation forces in Austria. Now in one of the world's best vacation spots, they lived in requisitioned houses and enjoyed fine food and recreation, swimming in the many lakes in the area, forming sports teams and enjoying baseball games, track teams and field meets.

They also had to continue the work of hunting down German soldiers, Nazis who had hidden out in this area hoping to keep up a fight, but the Rainbow men set up tight road patrols and made thorough searches of every hotel or cabin that could be a hideout for these remaining Nazis. As the Nazis were rounded up, they were put under control of German officers and, using German vehicles were taken to huge camps across the Austrian border in Germany.

Near the end of May the Rainbow Division began a training program to prepare them for possible deployment to the Pacific, although they hoped it would not necessary. They were taught Japanese tactics, as well as information programs and physical conditioning.

The next letter Forehand sent home was from Hoffgarten, Austria . . .

June 28, 1945

Dearest Sweethearts:

I received your sweet letter today of June 20. Surely glad you four were getting along okay. Hope my grown daughter keeps eating lots so she can be fat like Janice and Gerome. I'm all ok. Honey, I got my guitar back today, it's just like new, the man really did a good job fixing it, it sure sounds good with the new strings on it. Darling, you know I want to be with and the babies, I'd give anything to see my baby eating as you say she does, but I've no idea when I'll be there. But I'm most sure Gerome will be walking anyway, before I see her. Honey, I wrote airmail yesterday asking for some things, maybe this v-mail may get there first, so, please send me one large Vaseline hair tonic, one large size shaving lotion, my overseas cap, and some candy or cookies. Well, dear, I'll close, be sweet, write often.

Your loving hubby and daddy, BF
Good night and Sweet dreams.

Forehand writes again from Hoffgarten:

July 8

Dearest Wife and Babies:

Will answer your sweet letter of June 30 I rec'd last nite. Surely glad you four were getting along ok. This leaves me getting along just fine and dandy. Darling, I have 4 rolls of film, 2 of which will fit your Kodak (I hope), and if they won't maybe you can borrow a Kodak that fits them. I'll try and send them to you this week sometime. I have a real good box Kodak, but can't mail it home, it's considered lost, but I will take it home by next March I hope. I'm going near Salzburg tomorrow to stay for a while. This has surely been a long lonesome

day. Well sweet, I'll close. Write often.
Worlds of love, Daddy

Early in July the Rainbow received orders to move to Salzburg, which was already crowded with troops and refugees. They hated to leave the beautiful Tyrol area with its beauty and nice accommodations, but since the French were to take over control of the entire Tyrol, the Rainbow moved on to Salzburg. In Salzburg, Forehand and others in his section were put up in a two story home whose owner was serving in France at the time. The accommodations were more comfortable than they had expected and they were grateful for it.

Forehand writes again, this time from Salzburg.

July 16

Dearest Wife and Babies:
Wonder how you four are this hot day? Fine, I hope, as for me, I'm all ok. I'll bet it's awfully hot at home now, only wish I were there with you all, it seems as if I'll go crazy sometimes, when I think I've got to stay away from my babies and you 7 more months. I'd give anything to be there. Honey, the cake was very good, except that about 1/8 of it had started to mold, so maybe you ought not try to send another thick cake until the weather cools off a bit. The cakes Gerome sent me sure are good, I still have some of them yet, the crax Peggy and Janice sent me are still good and fresh too. I've not put my diamond strings on my guitar yet, it sounds good enough with the other strings you sent me. Honey, please get me one of each number (#) song books that Ernest Tubbs has made, including the one I had at home and send to me—he must have at least 3 song books and I want one of each. Also try to get me a banjo or mandolin "felt pick" and send to me. Well, honey, it's dinner time, I'll

close and go get it, so be sweet and write often.
Your loving hubby and daddy

A special ceremony was held by the Rainbow in the Residence Platz in Salzburg, during which the 250 men who remained of the First Battalion who had fought and lost so many men in the defense of Hatten, were awarded a Unit Citation. The ceremony was a celebration of the two year anniversary of the reactivation of the Rainbow Division, and the colorful flags of all the states were carried through the streets of Salzburg.

The Rainbow was also placed in charge of the huge task of cutting hundreds of thousands of meters of wood for winter fuel. They supervised thousands of prisoners of war to do the job, and it was a job that went through the rest of the summer and into the fall.

Even though the Allies had won the victory in Europe already, the Japanese still has not surrendered. On July 21, the United States delivered a final ultimatum to the Japanese to quit the war or face total destruction. On July 24 at the Potsdam conference in defeated Germany, President Harry Truman told Stalin, the communist dictator of the Soviet Union, that the United States had "a new weapon of unusual destructive force." On July 29 the Japanese formally rejected the U.S. ultimatum.

A week later, on August 6, the world's first atomic bomb (uranium) named Little Boy, was dropped on Hiroshima, Japan, from the Enola Gay, a B-29 bomber piloted by Col. Tibbets of the 509th Composite group, the first military unit in history to drop a nuclear bomb in combat.

On August 8, the Soviet Union declared war on Japan, and on August 9, the world's second atomic bomb, the Fat Man, was dropped on Nagasaki, Japan from a B-29 bomber piloted by Major Charles W. Sweeney. On August 14, Emperor Hirohito announced Japan's defeat to his people, and Japan accepted an unconditional surrender. Japanese Foreign Minister Mamoru Shigemitsu signed the surrender aboard the

U.S. Battleship Missouri in Tokyo Bay, Japan, on September 2, 1945. That day became known as V-J Day, Victory over Japan.

A week before the dropping of the first atomic bomb, Forehand had written an original birthday card to Hazel, hoping it would get to her before her birthday on August 16. Written in beautiful calligraphy script in his own hand, it read . . .

Your Birthday's coming soon, dear,

and though I'm far away,

I'll be thinking of you, my Darling Wife,

I would love to be with you this day.

But war has drawn me far from you,

it seems I've left you so long,

You've been a sweet little mother to our babies

since I have been gone.

I remember the night I kissed you,

and left you standing in the door.

I've been with you each night, dear, in dreamland,

I've missed you more than you'll ever know.

I've spent many nights in my foxhole,

sleeping in snow, mud and rain,

Praying for God to help me to live,

to be with my loved ones again.

It's over now, and I'm still living,

though we're thousands of miles apart,

I'm sending my love and best wishes,

Happy Birthday to you, Sweetheart.

Yours till the end, Buck

And writing again from Krimml, Austria on a photo postcard of a large house he says:

> August 6, '45
>
> Honey, this is the Gasthaus where I'm staying. There's 54 men in my platoon and this house accommodates all of us fine. I've a private room, all nicely furnished.
>
> Yours, Buck

CHAPTER TWENTY-TWO

Dreams Come True

Now that the war was finally over, and the Pacific preparations no longer necessary, to their great relief, the Rainbow Division stops further training and begins plans to return to the states. It won't happen quickly, as there are thousands upon thousands of soldiers to transport back to the U.S. and it will require many ships to get them all back home. The U.S. Government came up with a points system of choosing which soldiers would be shipped home first, the points based on time in service, time overseas, time in combat, and number of children. It seemed a fair way to handle the huge task of getting all the soldiers home again, those with the highest points would be sent home first.

Now serving as occupation forces in Austria, the Rainbow Division continues assigned duties , but also have some free time in which they can see some of the countryside of Europe. Three-day passes were easy to request, so Forehand and a number of his unit took the train to Paris to enjoy a little sightseeing. In Paris they stayed in the Hotel Atlantic, which the U.S. Government had leased to house servicemen on leave. They made the tour around the city, taking photos and seeing all the famous sites including the Eiffel Tower and the Arc de Triomphe.

Forehand enjoyed the history and beauty of the city, but excluded himself from the invitation of wine and women; some of his buddies who accepted the temptation ended up visiting the medical clinic and undergoing treatment upon their arrival back in Austria. He bought some souvenirs in Paris, including a replica of the Eiffel Tower, pretty silk embroidered postcards to send his girls and wife, and the beautiful yellow silk pouch in which Hazel kept his letters after she received the package.

In Austria, some of the Rainbow's occupational duties included feeding displaced persons, guarding supplies and military installations and even art treasures. And although some units set up classes of study for the men to help further along their education, soon some of the men, those with the highest points, began shipping out for home, and their numbers were replaced with around 5000 men from the 66th

Infantry Division, the men with lower points who would be waiting longer for their trip home. General Collins welcomed the new men into the Rainbow Division, saying that the Rainbow was proud to have been a part of winning the war, but would also be proud to be a part of winning the peace as occupation forces.

After having moved to another location in Austria, Forehand writes from Linz . . .

October 24

My Darling Ones!
Will ans your sweet letter I rec'd last nite, of Oct. 12. This leaves me getting along just fine. hope you four are still getting along good. Honey, I had a dream of you last nite, and I wanta see you so bad, I dreamed you were so beautiful and lovely, that I wanted to marry you. What do you think of a dream like that? Guess I dreamed of you because when I lay down, I was thinking of the good times that we are gonna have when I'm back again. Well, we won't have to get married again, but we're gonna have another honeymoon, or do you wanta go honeymooning with me? And would you mind if we allow three more beautiful girls to go with us? I think an awful lot of these three girls, but we can take them along and still do the things (you and I) we want to do, we could enjoy ourselves much better if we take them along, anyway. Well, Honey! I have no news as to whether we'll ship out on schedule or not, but division headquarters are leaving today, so I'm most sure we'll leave Nov. 3rd. Only hope we sail when we're supposed to, I sure wanta be with you four for Christmas, and all I ask the army to do is get me across the Atlantic, and to the states by Dec. 20. I'll be with you four for Christmas furlough or no furlough, that's the intentions of every man I've talked to. I'll bet there will be many men home for Christmas without passes this year. The shipping

situation is getting better, in mid-November there'll be 6 or 7 aircraft carriers moving troops to the states. One of them is the Enterprise, maybe I'll get to ride Willie's old ship home, any old thing to get me across the pond. I'm still wondering where we are gonna make our home. I still think that we'll make a trip down around St. Petersburg or possibly Miami, looking for a place to settle down. It's been kindly rainy for the last day or so, and I sure do get blue nothing to do but lay around and think of you four and the home we hope to have some day. I go to the movies most every afternoon or evening. Honey, I don't understand why you're not hearing from me, but you know how the mail gets messed up. I write as often as I can think of enough to write about. I'm sure glad Leroy got you some good firewood. Well, Dear, I'm out of news, so I'll stop. Write often,

Your loving PFC, Daddy

Forehand's last letter home is written in Camp Pittsburgh, in Rheims, France, the same city in which Germany surrendered to the Allies. It is the last letter he will write before boarding ship in LeHavre for his long-awaited trip home.

November 10, 1945

My Darling Wife and Babies:
Will write you a few more lines to let you know I'm still ok, hope you four are still ok. Well, Honey, I'm still doing something that the other fellows are not doing. I'm still writing to you all, just because they think they're gonna be home in about 30 or 40 days, they are not gonna write anymore, but I'll keep on writing to you as long as I'm away from you. I read in the Stars and Stripes yesterday that the 26th Division had been given a ready date for December 10. But even at that date, I can still be home by Dec. 20, and you can

continue planning on me being home for Christmas. All we're doing today is getting our records checked, taking short arms (medical check for VD), and all that kind of stuff. The last letter I had from you was written Oct. 25th, but I'm sure it's not your fault, it's just that we are doing lots of moving around and mail just isn't catching up with us. But I don't mind not getting letters from you as long as it's because I'm en route to see you. We have a heater inside our tent and it stays real hot all day, as it's plenty cold here. I have a pretty bad cold, I took a flu shot day before yesterday and it's had me aching all over ever since, but I can tell I'm improving. I still have my guitar, and if nothing happens, I'll take it home with me, and if you still want me to, I'll play you a tune, and if you don't want me to, well, I imagine I'll play it anyhow. I don't know whether I'll go to Brussels or not, it's a pretty rough ride in this cold cloudy weather. Well, Honey, you may as well stop writing to me when you get this, they'll not catch up with me. You can tell the ladies that you're not gonna write to Dada any more, he's coming home. I'll write again soon, be sweet, I'll see you Christmas.

Worlds of love, Dada

Only a few days later, sure enough, Forehand and his Division boarded the USS India Victory, a Liberty ship, in LeHavre for the return trip to the states. They were marched into a hold on the ship, told "This is where you sleep", and they put their bags down. The hold was so crowded that when they all lay down, they were so close to each other they could hardly roll over. They were served two meals every day, a late breakfast and an early supper, and spent most of their time laying down resting, most of them seasick. Late one afternoon as the ship rocked along in rough waters, Forehand became so seasick that he needed to vomit, but, not being able to get past the other men on the floor, he swallowed the vomit rather than throw up on the men around him.

Since they did not have to zigzag on the voyage home, no longer worried about enemy subs, the trip was several days shorter than the trip over had been. But the seas were rough, and as the ship ploughed through the waves, even though they were free to walk the deck, most of the men spent the greater part of the day in their quarters, counting the days till they would arrive at the home port and get their feet back on solid ground.

Their excitement grew as they approached the shores of home, then sailed up the Hudson River to their discharge pier, then on from there to Camp Miles Standish in Massachusetts. The men were sent by train to their various parts of the country, as near as they could go to their homes, then went on by bus or any other way they could go.

Forehand rode a train back to Camp Blanding, where he received his honorable discharge papers on December 1, then took a bus to the bus station nearest home. He unloaded his gear off the bus, then paid a two dollar taxi fare to take him the twenty miles to the little house where Hazel and the three ladies—or babies—awaited him.

The taxi pulled up in front of the little country house and waited as Forehand unloaded his belongings. He picked up his guitar and walked up onto the little porch playing and singing, which quickly brought Hazel running to the door. He had never been so happy as he was to see her

and the three little girls who now woke up to meet their Daddy. That night they all five slept together . . . so glad to be a family again, their soldier safely home from the war. And as they all had hoped, he was home for Christmas.

CHAPTER TWENTY-THREE

Life After the War

True to his dreams and plans, Berlie went looking for a place to build the home he had sketched in one of his letters, and with the help of his father and brothers, built the house. Rather than relocating farther away in Central or South Florida, he bought five acres on the outskirts of Panama City in the city of Callaway. And after enjoying a warm family Christmas, so different from the previous Christmas he had spent in France on the frontline exchanging gunfire with the Germans and standing guard duty, Berlie began construction of the house on the first day of 1946. It was just wonderful to be home once again with his wife and girls, and he was excited to be working on the house he had been planning in his mind for the last year. Only a few weeks later, on February 18, Berlie moved his family into their new home, although they did not have electricity for over a year. In December of that same year, yet another daughter was born, their fourth, who is the author of this book.

Berlie returned to the civilian work force as a heavy-duty mechanic on military equipment at the Navy Mine defense Laboratory at Panama City Beach, a job he held for twenty years before he retired.

Being ambitious to provide well for his family and enjoying the challenge of doing so, Berlie acquired another five-acre tract of land a short distance away from the house they had recently completed, and decided to build yet another home on the new property. It was completed enough to move into by November of 1947, after which they did the finish work. During the years that followed, Berlie made several additions on the house, from enlarging the kitchen and dining areas, to adding another bath, screened porch, garage, and even two more bedrooms and a bath upstairs as the five children grew and they required more room. A steady flow of friends kept Hazel and the girls working in the kitchen, and Berlie often invited their pastor and visiting ministers and missionaries to their home for lunch on Sundays.

Besides his eight-hour work days at the Navy Base, Berlie decided to build some apartments and mobile home park on the five acres behind their home. He did most of the work himself after arriving home from his job every day, often stopping in the house only long enough to drop off his lunch box and kiss the cook before heading out the back door to get back to work on his current project, whether it was digging foundations, framing up apartments, or laying plumbing and sewer. When he needed help, he often hired tenants to work with him. Most of the tenants were young Air Force families who were stationed at nearby Tyndall Air Force Base.

Understanding firsthand what it was like to be far away from home and family, Berlie, with Hazel's help and cooking expertise, organized holiday barbecues and parties for the families who rented the mobile homes and nine apartments. Many of the young Air Force wives came to Hazel for advice or just a friendly chat, and when they relocated to other bases or left the Air Force life for civilian live, they sent letters and Christmas cards thanking Hazel and Berlie for their kindness, for providing them a home away from home.

In February of 1949, Berlie and Hazel finally welcomed their first, and only, son into the family, named Douglas Gerald but called Jerry. Now Berlie could enjoy doing some Christmas shopping for boy things like wagons and BB guns and fishing rods; and when Jerry was only nine or ten years old and could barely peep over the steering wheel, Berlie allowed him to drive his truck around the circles of the trailer park when he was helping him work.

All the children helped with chores around the house and also in the trailer park and apartments, whether it was mowing grass or raking straw, painting or scrubbing, or just holding the other end of the board that Berlie was sawing for his construction. There was always something to do, and Berlie and Hazel believed in teaching their children to be efficient at a number of things. But they also believed in taking time to go on picnics to Sandy Creek or to the Jetties at the beach. Or piling into the back of Berlie's pickup truck with a bundle of fishing poles and crickets and earthworms for an all-day fishing trip to the Chipola River or Dead Lakes a half-hour's drive away.

Berlie and Hazel were also faithful church members and both of them were involved in Church leadership, Berlie serving as a deacon for many years and Hazel as a Sunday School teacher and Women's where in france

Dearest Sweethearts,
Friday Nite March 2, 1945

Wonder how my four girls are getting along to nite? fine I hope re/ as for me, I'm all ok, its pretty cold here again, snowing a bit, but don't look for a heavy snow, now,

I'm doing nothing but lying around, and as you can see, doing a bit of Post-War Planning, decided to send plans to you and let you see the house "were gona build" I hope, what you think of the plans its long time off, but maby well get to it, by & buy and things sure it gona be a long ways from Kindred, I'm gona build it my self, with the help of Hazel Peggy Janice & Jerome, ofC. I am still xoo you, Peggy & my self as we built the little shack you're living in now,

Well thats I'm sleepy so I'le stop, hoping to hear from you all soon,

so take care of yours all and our three little daughters, your loving bully & daddy,

Girls Love Daddy

182

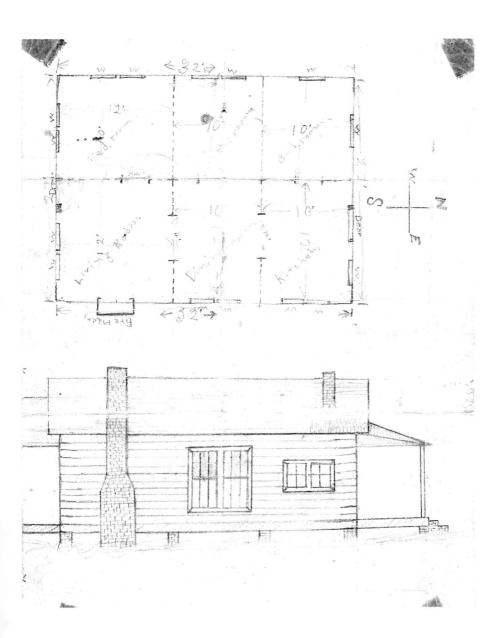

Ministries leader as well. Her favorite friends were the group of ladies she met with weekly to stitch quilts, which they did together for a number of years.

Berlie rarely mentioned his war experiences, at least not to his family; and although he brought home a number of interesting mementos from Europe, he kept them packed safely away for the most part. Maybe as time passed and he became busily engaged in earning a living and raising a family, the war was also packed away on a shelf in his mind. It now seemed so far away—which, of course, it was—and so long ago, which it really wasn't, that Berlie decided to put it behind him and get on with what he lived through the war to do, and that was simply to go on with life.

But war changes a man. When a man becomes part of the war, the war becomes part of the man, remains part of the man, and helps make him a better man, in most cases. At least that is what it did for Berlie. He seemed to realize how lucky he was to have made it back home to the family that meant so much to him. He knew that many of his fellow soldiers were not allowed that privilege, and he was grateful that he was not one of those who had not made it home. He had seen over and over again, during the time he had spent on the front, just how quickly a life could come to an end. Sure he had been plenty afraid a few times, when the prospect of being hit or killed was as likely as it was for any other guy around him; but he had made it through the war without a single injury. No purple heart for him, but his heart was still beating, and for that he was thankful.

Berlie was a true patriot; he loved his country and was glad he had been given the opportunity to fight for the freedom he loved. As the years of his life passed from one decade into another, his appreciation for America did not dim but grew ever stronger. He loved the Stars and Stripes and all things American, he enjoyed singing the anthems and hymns of the beauty of America, and he didn't mind the responsibilities that came with the rights. He had fought on her side, the fight had been long and difficult, and the losses had been steep. He had heard things and seen things he would never forget, not even if he lived to be a hundred. But he also knew how to put the things behind him that were over and done with, and to make the best of the time he had been given. So he packed away, on the shelves of his mind, the things that had bothered him, frightened him, and angered him, and he made up his mind to long let those things make him a better man than he might have been without having experienced them.

And Hazel packed away, in the bottom of the cedar chest in their bedroom, the yellow silk pouch of letters Berlie had sent to her from France, Germany, and Austria. She passed the cedar chest on to Peggy when she got married in the 60s, but took the silk pouch of letters and tucked them away again. They remained her secret, and perhaps it was in the last years of her life, as her health began to fail, that she placed them in the bottom drawer of her dresser, where her children would be sure to find them when she was gone. They wondered if she could have imagined how excited they would be to discover them, or how much it would mean to them, and especially to Berlie, to know that she had kept the letters all those years—the letters from Dada, her Rainbow Soldier.

EPILOGUE

Rainbow Never Forget

When I was only a young girl, eight or ten years old, a large dark blue hardback book caught my eye on a shelf in my Dad and Mother's bedroom. I picked it up, sat down to look it over, and was shocked and frightened by some of the photos. They were photos of holocaust victims in the concentration camp in Germany known as Dachau. My young mind could not comprehend what those photos meant; I only knew they saddened me and left me with a lot of questions—questions I didn't have the courage to ask my Dad at the time. Dad simply didn't talk about those things, and even then I felt it was because he was protecting me from things that were too unbearable for me in my happy world of childhood. The blue book was the combat history of the 42nd Infantry Division, and after seeing me visibly worried about those photos, either my Dad or my Mother placed the book farther out of my reach. It was years later that the story found in those pages came to life in my mind as I finally read the blue book. I knew my Dad had been in World War II, though he hardly ever mentioned it. As I followed the trail of the 42nd Infantry "Rainbow" Division from their landing in Marseilles, through the descriptions of their battles in France and Germany, I began to feel acquainted with the soldiers of the 42nd.

Near the end of the blue book is a two-page spread of a few 42nd ID soldiers throwing snowballs and rolling in the snow in Austria while they were serving as Occupational Forces after the war ended in 1945. One of the men in the photo is identified—in Dad's handwriting—as "Sarge Owen from Oklahoma City".

Sixty-two years later, in July of 2007, Dad and Sarge Arnold Owen met again, face-to-face, in a hotel meeting room in Virginia Beach at the annual reunion of the Rainbow Division Veterans Memorial Foundation. Sarge Owen walked up to Dad and said in his soft Oklahoma drawl: "Burl, do you remember me?" Then after only a few seconds, he added "I'm the guy that busted your guitar." Dad's blue eyes widened and a big grin spread across his face as he responded "Sarge Owen?" From that moment they renewed a friendship that had slept between the pages of the blue book for almost sixty-two years, and the two of them spent a lot of time over the next few days enjoying catching up on each others lives and reminiscing about events from the war. It was amazing to see that the bond forged between them on the battlefields of Europe was still intact after all those years. Dad's enjoyment was evident as he renewed acquaintances with other men of the 42nd with whom he had served; and on the last evening of the reunion, Sarge's daughter-in-law Linda persuaded Dad to dance with her as a military band played a World War II era song.

That was the last time Dad danced, as less than two years later he had a leg amputated due to poor circulation. He got to see Sarge Owen only once after the Virginia Beach Reunion, when we took him to the big Veteran's Day celebration that is held yearly in Birmingham, Alabama. Dad delighted in the activities there, being with all the Top Brass in uniform, and especially participating in the grand Veteran's Day Parade, in the bus filled with 42nd Division veterans and their spouses and family members, waving their flags at the windows and smiling at the cheering crowds along the parade route.

Dad was unable to attend any more reunions, but my husband Henry and I, as well as my sister Fran and our grandson Marcus, have attended other reunions and had the pleasure of getting to know other Rainbowmen who marched across Europe with Dad and Sarge Owen—men like Elmer Kohrt, Richard Kesl, and Joseph Popio. Although he normally walked, "Popio from Ohio," as the men had called him, allowed me the honor of pushing him in a wheelchair through the beautiful military museum at Wright Patterson Air Force Base in Dayton, Ohio.

Popio had been my Dad's jeep driver during the war, and now I was driving him around, a joyous reversal of roles which we both laughed about. These men, and all the Veterans of the 42nd Infantry, along with their lovely wives who wrote letters and sent packages of goodies to them to help keep their morale high on the battlefield, have truly won my respect and affection. Sadly, in the few short years we have known them, a number of these wonderful men of the WWII

42nd Infantry have "passed over the Rainbow", among them Elmer Kohrt and Sarge Arnold Owen.

But the 42nd Infantry Rainbow Division doesn't end with these gentlemen veterans from World War II. When the war in Europe was over, and after serving as occupational forces in Austria, the 42nd was inactivated in June of 1946. The following year, in 1947, the 42nd became a National Guard Division for New York, the state in which the Rainbow Division was first formed in 1917. In the decades since 1947, the 42nd has worn the Rainbow Infantry patch as responders in numerous emergencies ranging from natural disasters such as blizzards, hurricanes, tornadoes, snowstorms and floods, to serving as volunteers in the Gulf War. In 1992 the Division became multistate. With the Headquarters located in Troy, New York, major portions of the Division were formed in New Jersey, Massachusetts, Vermont, Delaware and Rhode Island. When the World Trade Center was attacked by terrorists in 2001, Rainbow battalions as part of Joint Task Force 42, immediately went into action as emergency responders sustaining security and recovery operations around Ground Zero.

In the global War on Terror, Rainbow soldiers have deployed to both Iraq and Afghanistan as well as uantanamo Bay Naval Base, Cuba. In 2004, the 42nd Division mobilized its first elements for Operation Iraqi Freedom. Hundreds of New York and New Jersey soldiers from the 42nd Division Artillery performed

Security duties in Iraq, and nearly 700 Rainbow soldiers serving with the division's 1st Battalion, 69th Infantry conducted combat operations as part of Task force Baghdad.

In 2004 more than 3,000 Rainbow soldiers from the division's Headquarters and base units led elements from more than 29 states as part of the Multinational Corps-Iraq, providing stability and support to the emerging Iraqi democratic government. Because of all the attached active and reserve units the Headquarters 42nd Division was also known as Task Force Liberty, based in Tikrit, Iraq on the site of a former presidential compound for Saddam Hussein. The 42nd led a Task Force comprised of more than 23,000 soldiers from the Army's

3rd Infantry division's 1st and 3rd Brigade Combat Teams, the Idaho Army National Guard's 116th Brigade Combat Team and the 278th Regimental Combat Team from the Tennessee Army National Guard. In Iraq, Rainbow soldiers conducted raids and combat actions, seized weapons caches, destroyed improvised explosive devices, and trained Iraqi Army forces. They also worked on reconstruction to ensure free elections for the Iraqi people.

A Brigade size element of Rainbow soldiers deployed again in late 2007 and in 2008 to Afghanistan to train Afghan Army and Police forces, in support of Operation Enduring Freedom.

The 42nd Division continues today as a multi-state National Guard Division, continuing to serve state and nation. Since its formation 95 years ago, the soldiers of the Rainbow have made America proud of their service and grateful for the sacrifices they have made to keep us free and to keep us safe. The motto of the 42nd is "Rainbow, Never Forget!". It's fitting that we the people should remember them and extend to them, and to all of our Military forces who serve around the globe, our gratitude for going where we could not go, and for doing what we could not do. **Rainbow, Never Forget!**

HISTORY

42nd Infantry Division

The 42nd Infantry (Rainbow) Division's history as a unit began with America's entry into World War I. Amidst the rush by America to mobilize, individual states competed with each other for the honor to be the first to send their national guard units to fight in the trenches of Europe. To check the negative implications of this competition and to minimize the impact the mobilization could have on any one state, the government decided to create a division composed of hand-picked national guard units from 26 states and the District of Columbia. As a result of this unified effort, the 42nd Infantry Division was born in August and organized in September of 1917 at Camp Mills on Long Island, New York.

Col. Douglas McArthur, who helped form the Division, said afterwards, "The 42nd Division stretches like a rainbow from one end of America to the other," and the name Rainbow stuck with the division.

The 42nd Division arrived in France in November 1917, and entered the front line March 1918, where it remained in almost constant contact with the enemy for 174 days. During its time in France, the 42nd Division participated in six major campaigns, and incurred one out of sixteen casualties suffered by the American Army during the war. The 42nd Division's service officially came to an end in May 1919.

With the onset of America's participation in World War II, the 42nd Division was reactivated. At the July 1943 reactivation ceremony, the new Division Commander, Brigadier General Harry Collins echoed McArthur's sentiment on the 42nd's unique status, saying " The Rainbow represents the people of our country".

The 42nd Division landed in France in December 1944 and as part of the 7th Army advanced through France and entered Germany in March of 1945. It was during the 42nd's rapid advance through Germany in April 1945 that they, along with the Guard's 45th Infantry Division, liberated the infamous Dachau concentration camp. By the end of the war, the 42nd Division had established an enviable record. It was first in its corps to enter Germany, first to penetrate the Siegfried Line and first into Munich. Rainbow soldiers had seized over 6000 square miles of Nazi held territory during their march across Europe. The Division ended the war serving as occupation forces in Austria, and was inactivated in June 1946.

UPDATE ON RAINBOW

The 42nd Division returned in 1947 as a national guard division and was recognized as a component of the New York Army National Guard.

Their headquarters was moved from New York City to Troy, New York, where it is today. In 1993, the 42nd was consolidated with elements of the 26th and 50th Divisions to form one national guard unit—now in the following states: New York, Vermont, New Jersey, Massachusetts, Connecticut, Delaware, Rhode Island, and New Mexico.

During World War II, the Rainbow Division spent 106 days in combat. Of the Rainbow soldiers: 333 were killed in combat, 1800 wounded, 1459 missing, 6 captured—total battle casualties were 3598, total non-battle casualties were 2351, and total casualties were 5949, (these statistics from internet site: www.WWII-v-mail).

Other websites used for information: Homepage of the 42nd Infantry Division, Rainbow Division Vet. Assoc., www.bunt.com/mconrad, and www.collegiate-va.org/khurd/wwii.htm (good one), also check National Archives and Records Administration at webmaster@nara. gov., and U.S. Library of Congress.

OTHER INFORMATION FOUND ABOUT 42ND RAINBOW DIVISION:

THE RAINBOW PATCH—three stripe rainbow shape, red on top, yellow center, blue on bottom—the patches were made by seamstresses on Long Island and later in France throughout WWI.

IN THE WWII 42ND RAINBOW DIVISION, the three infantry regiments were numbered 222nd, 232nd, and 242nd, (Dad's was 242nd)—there were other units as well, field artillery, etc.

IN THE AUTUMN OF 1944, the three infantry regiments were rushed overseas ahead of the remainder of the Division. They were designated as "Task Force Linden" and as one infantryman said, they were "flung into the maw", totally fragmented, segregated with no artillery or backup support to bolster other thinned-down divisions trying to prevent a breakout of two German armies in Alsace. Task Force Linden's companies were used to defend against and attack and counterattack powerful German forces along a 30 mile furious battlefront in Jan. 1945. The rest of the division arrived in France in January 1945 and the division was at last intact. The Rainbow Division as part of the expanded 7th Army attacked through the strong German defensive positions in the Hardt mountains of France, penetrated the Siegfried Line at the German frontier, crossed the Rhine, and advanced into the cradle of Nazism, capturing Wurzburg, Schweinfurt, Furth (Nuremburg's twin city), Donauworth, liberating Dachau concentration camp on April 29, 1945, and swept through Munich on April 30, shortly before the war ended on May 8.

LOOK FOR THESE BOOKS:

THE RAINBOW LIBERATION MEMORIES
Dachau 29 April 1945

THE FINAL CRISIS A Combat History of WWII, 42nd Rainbow Infantry Division, edited by Lt. Col. Hugh C. Daly, 1946.

Further information from internet sources:

ABOUT THE LIBERATION OF PRISONERS AT DACHAU

As important as the liberation itself was the aftermath, there were over 30,000 dazed and ravaged inmates. The Rainbow was charged with their welfare. Thanks to the sympathy, understanding, and humane efforts of our officers and man, most of the survivors were delivered from near death to full life.

Almost half of the American soldiers there were only 18, 19, or 20 years old, and were horrified at what they saw —the soldiers sat with and wept with the victims. Major Gen. Harry J. Collins (Rainbow's Commanding officer) was so deeply moved by the experience at Dachau , he went far beyond the requirements of duty. Because of his compassion, the survivors received aid the U.S. Army was able to supply, including even kosher foods, religious articles, money, etc. They, the Rainbow, were eyewitness to the Holocaust—a day of shock, horror and liberation.

MORE NOTES OF INTEREST FROM INTERNET SOURCES:

THE 42ND RAINBOW INFANTRY DIVISION TOOK 59,128 PRISONERS OF WAR

They were awarded (to individuals) 185 silver stars, and 515 bronze stars, among other medals of honor.

ARRIVING IN MARSEILLES,

they pitched pup tents in pouring rain.

ALL THE ARMY STAGING CAMPS IN LEHAVRE FRANCE

were named after cigarettes: Camp Lucky Strike, Camp Philip Morris, etc.

AFTER THE WAR ENDED, a musical about the service of the Rainbow Division was presented for several months in a theater in Salzburg, Austria, the musical was "Glory Road".

CHRISTMAS EVE, DURING THE BATTLE OF THE BULGE, the German U-boat U-486 sunk the ship Leopoldville while carrying the 66th Infantry Division across the English Channel. Men were not wearing life jackets; of the 2200 aboard, almost 1000 were killed or drowned.

DAD'S WAR LISTING OF SHIPS THAT CARRIED TROOPS TO AND FROM WAR, Dad's 42nd Division is listed on the wrong ship over; says USS Mount Vernon, landing in Marseille 11/13/44. My father remembers it was the USS William S. Black and the dates on his letters "at sea" begin November 30, '44. Contact Corporal Ivan Louis Tominack (7th Army, 42nd I.D., 445th Ordnance, HAM Company.

Nobody knows why—IN 1951, THE DEPT. OF ARMY DESTROYED all ship passenger lists, logs of vessels, manifests, and troop movement files of U.S. Army transport for WWI.

DAD'S SHIP OVER—USS General William S. Black, and ship back was USS India Victory, which disembarked in New York—to Camp Kilmer, New Jersey, on Hudson River.

ABOUT LIBERATION OF DACHAU 30,000 men, women, and children representing over 30 nationalities, were liberated that day. Another 4000 corpses were also found in 40 boxcars on the railroad that served the camp—they had been sent from Buchenwald to Dachau, with no food—only one single man was found alive in the 40 boxcars.

THE MAGINOT LINE (Dad mentions being in a pillbox here) was the line of heavy fortifications the French built on their border after WWI.

EVENTS ALREADY PASSED BEFORE DAD ARRIVED IN FRANCE: Allies had already bombed Berlin (launched air offensive from Britain , crippling German air power (Jan.-May 44).

JUNE 6, 44—INVASION OF NORMANDY Allied forces under Eisenhower storm the Normandy coast (Operation Overlord) and sweep across France. Aug. 25, Paris liberated, then allies proceed to Austria and Germany.

EVENTS HAPPENING AS DAD ARRIVES SOUTHERN FRANCE:

DEC. 16-26, 1944—BATTLE OF THE BULGE The Germans counterattack against U.S. troops in Belgium. After pushing 50 mines into Belgium, the Germans are checked at Bastogne.

FARTHER ON:

MARCH 7 THRU MAY 8, 45—FALL OF GERMANY From the west, Eisenhower's army pushes into Germany and overruns its industrial heartland. From the east, the Russian army takes Warsaw and crosses into Germany. On April 25, American and Russian troops meet at Torgau on the Elbe. Berlin falls on May 2, and on May 8, Germany surrenders (V-E Day).

*The Rainbow Reveille newspaper reporting on the
42nd Honoring V-E Day in May 11, 1945.*

CPSIA information can be obtained at www.ICGtesting.com
Printed in the USA
LVOW13s1804270514

387449LV00001B/256/P